Personal taxation 2012/13

Workbook

for Finance Act 2012 assessments

Aubrey Penning

Bob Thomas

osborne BOOKS

Published by Osborne Books Limited
Unit 1B Everoak Estate
Bromyard Road
Worcester WR2 5HP
Tel 01905 748071
Email books@osbornebooks.co.uk
Website www.osbornebooks.co.uk

Design by Laura Ingham
Cover and page design image © Istockphoto.com/Petrovich9

Printed by CPI Antony Rowe Limited, Chippenham

British Library Cataloguing in Publication Data
A catalogue record for this book is available from the British Library

ISBN 978 1905777 952

Contents

Acknowledgements

The publisher wishes to thank the following for their help with the reading and production of the book: Maz Loton, Jon Moore and Cathy Turner. Thanks are also due to Laura Ingham for her designs for this series.

The publisher is indebted to the Association of Accounting Technicians for its kind permission for the reproduction of its sample assessment in this text.

Author and Technical Editor

Aubrey Penning, the author, has previously co-ordinated the AAT courses at Worcester College of Technology, and taught a range of units including Management Accounting and the two taxation Units. He has over twenty years experience of teaching accountancy on a variety of courses in Worcester and Gwent. He is a Certified Accountant, and before his move into full-time teaching he worked for the health service, a housing association and a chemical supplier. Aubrey is author of *Business Taxation*, *Budgeting* and *Financial Performance* and co-author of *Basic Costing* and *Cash Management*, all published by Osborne Books.

Bob Thomas, the Technical Editor of this book, has been involved with the Education and Training activities of the AAT since 1986, including the development and piloting of the skills-based scheme. He is an external verifier, a simulation writer, a moderator and a contributor at workshops, training days, conferences and master classes. Until recently he was a member of the Learning and Development Board and Chairman of the Assessment Panel.

Introduction

what this book covers

This book has been written specifically to cover Learning Area 'Personal Tax' which combines two QCF Units in the AAT Level 4 Diploma in Accounting:

■   Principles of personal tax

■   Calculating personal tax

This book has been designed to include guidance and exercises based on Tax Year 2012/13 (Finance Act 2012). We understand that the AAT plan to assess this legislation from January 2013 to December 2013. Tutors and students are advised to check this with the AAT and ensure that they sit the correct Computer Based Assessment.

what this book contains

This book is set out in two sections:

■   **Chapter activities** which provide extra practice material in addition to the activities included in the Osborne Books Tutorial text. Answers to the Chapter activities are set out in this book.

■   **Practice assessments** are included to prepare the student for the Computer Based Assessments. They are based directly on the structure, style and content of the sample assessment material provided by the AAT at www.aat.org.uk. Suggested answers to the Practice Assessments are set out in this book.

online support from Osborne Books

This book is supported by practice material available at www.osbornebooks.co.uk

This material is available to tutors – and to students at their discretion – in two forms:

■   A **Tutor Zone** which is available to tutors who have adopted the Osborne Books texts. This area of the website provides extra assessment practice material (plus answers) in addition to the activities included in this Workbook text.

■   **Online learning** – online practice questions designed to familiarise students with the style of the AAT Computer Based Assessments.

   Scan the code on the right using your Smartphone to gain access to the online practice questions.

further information

If you want to know more about our products, please visit www.osbornebooks.co.uk, email books@osbornebooks.co.uk or telephone Osborne Books Customer Services on 01905 748071.

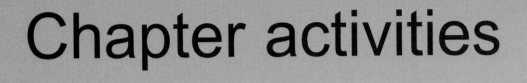

Chapter activities

Chapter activities

1 **Introduction to income tax**

1.1 State whether each of the following statements is true or false.

✓

		True	False
(a)	An individual's tax records only need to be kept until one year after the end of the tax year, unless an investigation is being carried out.	✓	
(b)	It is not the taxpayer's responsibility to inform HMRC of any untaxed taxable income, unless they have been asked to complete a tax return.		✓
(c)	Accountants must normally follow the rules of confidentiality, but there are exceptions.	✓	
(d)	Where a practitioner has knowledge or suspicion that his client is money laundering, then he has a duty to inform the relevant person or authority.	✓	
(e)	Accountants should warn clients if they suspect money laundering to give the client a chance to cease the activity.		✓
(f)	When an accountant is advising a client the greatest duty of care is to the client.	✓	

1.2 State which of the following can provide sources of information about tax law and its interpretation.

✓

		Yes	No
(a)	HMRC extra-statutory concessions	✓	
(b)	Statute law	✓	
(c)	HMRC statements of practice	✓	
(d)	Case law	✓	
(e)	Website www.hmrc.gov.uk	✓	
(f)	Website www.statistics.gov.uk		✓
(g)	HMRC guides and help sheets	✓	

1.3   Match the following examples of income with the correct income category.

Sample Income	Income Category
UK dividends	Property Income
Partnership profits	Savings and Investment Income
Rents from land	Trading Income
Earnings from a job	Employment, Pension and Social Security Income

1.4   Tick the columns to show which of the following categories of income is taxed on an accruals basis, and which is on a receipts basis (ie based on when received).

✓

Income Category	Accruals Basis	Receipts Basis
Property Income	✓	
Savings and Investment Income		✓
Trading Income	✓	
Employment, Pension and Social Security Income		✓

1.5   State which of the following types of income are exempt from income tax.

✓

Income Category	Exempt	Not Exempt
(a) Employment income		✓
(b) Income from an ISA	✓	
(c) Premium bond prizes	✓	
(d) Rent received from a buy-to-let property		✓
(e) Betting winnings (unless a professional gambler)	✓	
(f) Lottery prizes	✓	

2 Chapter activities
Income from property

2.1 Chester has two properties in addition to his home, details of which are as follows:

Two bedroom house:

(1) This unfurnished house is rented out for £850 per month. The property was occupied this tax year until 1 February when the tenants suddenly moved out, owing the rent for January. Chester knows that he will not recover this rent. The property was let again from 1 May to another family.

(2) Chester had to pay £530 for redecoration in March following the poor condition of the property at that time.

(3) The only other expense paid by Chester on the house was 10% management charge to the agent on rent received.

One bedroom flat:

(1) This furnished flat is rented out for £550 per month. The property was rented all tax year.

(2) Chester paid council tax and water rates on the flat, totalling £1,100 for the period that the flat was occupied. He also paid buildings and contents insurance of £340 for the year.

Calculate the profit or loss made on each property, using the following table.

	Two bedroom house £	One bedroom flat £
Income		
Expenses:		

2.2 Select the statements that are true from the following ✓

	True	False
(a) The maximum amount of gross rent that can be received tax free under the rent a room scheme is £5,250.		
(b) The rent a room scheme only applies to furnished accommodation.		
(c) Rent a room relief can be claimed for guest houses provided it is also the claimant's main residence.		
(d) Taxpayers can claim both rent a room relief and wear and tear allowance for the same property.		
(e) Eligible taxpayers do not have to claim rent a room relief if they choose not to.		
(f) Rent a room relief can only be claimed by owner-occupiers.		
(g) Charges for goods or services like food or laundry are ignored when calculating the gross rent.		

2.3 Sienna owns a field where she has three static caravans that are rented out to holidaymakers. The caravans are available to the public for rent from 1 March to 31 October each year. This year, during this period there were three weeks when the caravans were unoccupied. Sienna carries out the caravan rentals on a commercial basis.

Select the statements that are true from the following: ✓

	True	False
(a) The rental of caravans qualifies as furnished holiday lettings		
(b) The rental of caravans is treated as a hobby and is exempt from tax		
(c) Although the caravans are furnished, wear and tear allowance cannot be claimed as these are holiday lettings		
(d) Interest on loans to buy the caravans can be claimed as allowable expenses		
(e) Rent a room relief can be claimed against the rental income		

2.4 Mahjabeen rents a furnished room in his own house to a lodger for £210 per week, including an evening meal. Heating the room costs Mahjabeen £150 for the year, and food for the lodger's meals costs £15 per week.

(i)   Calculate the assessable amount for the tax year, based on

    (a)   claiming rent a room relief, and

    (b)   preparing a normal rental income computation

    using the following table.

	Claiming rent a room relief £	Normal rental income computation £
Income	10,920	10,920
Allowable deductions		

(ii)   Complete the following sentence:

To pay the minimum income tax, Mahjabeen should **claim / not claim** rent a room relief.

2.5   Stephan rents out one furnished property. He claims wear and tear allowance. The following is a statement compiled from his accounting records relating to the tax year.

	£	£
Rental Income Receivable		12,000
less expenditure:		
Council Tax	700	
Water Rates	300	
Insurance	380	
Cost of replacement furniture	2,100	
Depreciation of furniture	800	
Managing Agent's Charges	1,200	
		5,480
Profit		6,520

Required

(a)   Calculate the assessable property income for Stephan, using the following table.

	£	£
Income		
Expenditure:		
Assessable Income		

(b)   Complete page UKP2 of the UK Property supplementary pages, (2011/12 version reproduced on the next page) for Stephan.

Property income

Do not include furnished holiday lettings, Real Estate Investment Trust or Property Authorised Investment Funds dividends/distributions here.

20 Total rents and other income from property

£ _____ · 0 0

21 Tax taken off any income in box 20

£ _____ · 0 0

22 Premiums for the grant of a lease – *from box E on the Working Sheet on page UKPN 8 of the notes.*

£ _____ · 0 0

23 Reverse premiums and inducements

£ _____ · 0 0

Property expenses

24 Rent, rates, insurance, ground rents etc.

£ _____ · 0 0

25 Property repairs, maintenance and renewals

£ _____ · 0 0

26 Loan interest and other financial costs

£ _____ · 0 0

27 Legal, management and other professional fees

£ _____ · 0 0

28 Costs of services provided, including wages

£ _____ · 0 0

29 Other allowable property expenses

£ _____ · 0 0

Calculating your taxable profit or loss

30 Private use adjustment – *read page UKPN 9 of the notes*

£ _____ · 0 0

31 Balancing charges – *read page UKPN 10 of the notes*

£ _____ · 0 0

32 Annual Investment Allowance

£ _____ · 0 0

33 Business Premises Renovation Allowance (Assisted Areas only) – *read page UKPN 11 of the notes*

£ _____ · 0 0

34 All other capital allowances

£ _____ · 0 0

35 Landlord's Energy Saving Allowance

£ _____ · 0 0

36 10% wear and tear allowance – *for furnished residential accommodation only*

£ _____ · 0 0

37 Rent a Room exempt amount

£ _____ · 0 0

38 Adjusted profit for the year – *from box O on the Working Sheet on page UKPN 16*

£ _____ · 0 0

39 Loss brought forward used against this year's profits

£ _____ · 0 0

40 Taxable profit for the year (box 38 minus box 39)

£ _____ · 0 0

41 Adjusted loss for the year – *from box O on the Working Sheet on page UKPN 16*

£ _____ · 0 0

42 Loss set off against 2011–12 total income – *this will be unusual – read page UKPN 15 of the notes*

£ _____ · 0 0

43 Loss to carry forward to following year, including unused losses brought forward

£ _____ · 0 0

Chapter activities

Income from savings and investments

3.1 Some taxable interest is received gross, and some is received net of 20% tax. Examine the following list of income sources, and analyse it into the way that interest is received, using the table.

- Loan stock from quoted company
- NS&I easy access savings account
- Local authority loan
- Treasury stock (a type of Gilt)
- Online building society account
- NS&I investment account

Received net	Received gross

3.2 During the tax year, Wesley received UK dividends of £900 and £480 interest from his NS&I investment account.

(i) What is the total amount of tax that is treated as already paid?

✓

(a)	None	
(b)	£345	
(c)	£220	
(d)	£100	

(ii) What is the total assessable income from these sources for the tax year?

✓

(a)	£1,380	
(b)	£1,480	
(c)	£1,725	
(d)	£1,600	

3.3   State which of the following sources provide tax-free (exempt) income:

	✓
(a) Government Stocks (Gilts)	
(b) UK Dividends	
(c) NS&I Index-linked Savings Certificates	
(d) Building Society Cash ISA	
(e) Bank ISA operated by post	
(f) Local Authority Loans	

3.4   Complete the following table to show the maximum investment in an ISA that an individual can make in 2012/13.

Total ISA limit	
Cash ISA limit	

Select from:
- (a)   £4,250
- (b)   £5,300
- (c)   £5,640
- (d)   £10,600
- (e)   £11,280

3.5   Katherine has received the amounts shown on the following table from various investments. Complete the table to show the assessable amounts and the amounts of tax that are treated as having been paid.

Investment	Amount Received £	Assessable Amount £	Tax treated as paid £
Bank Account	560		
UK Dividends	2,700		
Cash ISA	120		
NS&I fixed interest savings certificate	400		
Debenture interest	800		
Totals	4,580		

Chapter activities

4 Income from employment

4.1 Complete the following table by correctly matching the indicators as relating to employment or self-employment.

Indicators of Employment	Indicators of Self Employment

Indicators

- Choose work hours and invoice for work done
- Need to do the work yourself
- Told how, where and when to do work
- No risk of capital or losses
- Work for several people or organisations
- Decide yourself how, when and where to do work
- Can employ helper or substitute
- Employer provides equipment
- Risk own capital and bear losses from work that is not to standard
- Work set hours and paid regular wage with sick pay and holidays
- Usually work for one employer
- Provide own equipment

4.2 **(1)** What scale charge percentage would be applied for petrol cars with the following CO_2 emissions?

(a)　111 g/km

(b)　134 g/km

(c)　151 g/km

(d)　249 g/km

(2) Silvia was provided with a second hand car on 6 October 2012. It cost the company £8,000, but the list price of this car when bought new was £17,000. The car has a CO_2 emission of 168g/km, and has a diesel engine. The company pays for all running costs, except private fuel.

(a)　The cost of the car used in the benefit in kind computation is

£

(b)　The percentage used in the benefit in kind computation is

　　%

(c)　The assessable benefit for Silvia relating to the car for 2012/13 is

£

4.3 **(1)** When accommodation is purchased by an employer, what is the value of the property above which an additional benefit is applied?

	✓
£60,000	
£70,000	
£75,000	
£80,000	
£100,000	
£125,000	

(2) Would the following situations be treated as being job-related where no accommodation benefit arises?

		Yes	No
(a)	House provided for a vicar		
(b)	House provided by employer for accountant working for a housing association		
(c)	Flat in sheltered accommodation provided for an on-site care manager		

(3) Summer was provided with accommodation in the form of a flat that the employer purchased for £165,000. It is not job related. The flat has an annual value £9,300. Summer pays £200 per month towards the private use of the flat. Assume that the HMRC official interest rate is 4.00%. Her taxable benefit is:

✓

£6,900	
£9,300	
£10,500	
£15,900	

4.4 On 6 December 2012, Kevin was provided with a company loan of £6,000 on which he pays interest at 1.5% per annum. On 6 February 2013 Kevin repaid £2,000. The official rate of interest is 4.00%.

What is the benefit in kind for 2012/13 to the nearest £?

4.5 **(1)** Dee uses her own car for business travelling. During the tax year she travelled 11,500 business miles for which she was paid 50p per mile by her employer. The impact of this is:

		✓
(a)	She will have a taxable amount of £575.	
(b)	She will have a taxable amount of £875.	
(c)	She will claim an allowable expense of £875.	
(d)	She will claim an allowable expense of £575.	

(2) Eddie has an occupational pension scheme to which he contributes 5% of his salary. His employer contributes 6% of his salary. His salary was £28,400. The impact of this is:

		✓
(a)	His taxable salary will be increased by £1,704.	
(b)	His taxable salary will be reduced by £1,420.	
(c)	His taxable salary will be increased by £284.	
(d)	His basic rate band will be extended by £1,775.	

(3) Steve pays £300 per year in subscriptions to professional bodies. His employer reimburses him £180. The overall impact of this is:

		✓
(a)	No impact on tax.	
(b)	An allowable deduction of £120.	
(c)	A benefit of £180.	
(d)	An allowable deduction of £300.	

(4) Genna has a non-contributory occupational pension scheme. This means:

		✓
(a)	The employer pays a percentage of her salary into the scheme, but Genna does not.	
(b)	Genna pays a percentage of her salary into the scheme, but the employer does not.	
(c)	Only the Government pays a percentage of her salary into the scheme.	
(d)	Genna and the Government both pay a percentage of her salary into the scheme.	

5 Chapter activities
Preparing income tax computations

5.1   Richard, who is 82 years old, had income of £25,000 and received dividends of £1,215.

He paid £400 (net) to charities under the gift aid scheme.

Calculate his total income tax liability (ie before deduction of tax paid) for the tax year, using the table given below.

	£
Income	
Gross dividends	
Personal allowance	
Taxable income	

5.2 Select from the following statements, those which are correct.

✓

		True	False
(a)	Payments on account relating to a tax year are paid on 31 January in the tax year, and on 31 July following the tax year.		
(b)	The final payment of income tax relating to a tax year is paid on 31 October following the end of the tax year.		
(c)	If a taxpayer is late paying income tax then he will either be subject to a penalty or interest, but not both.		
(d)	If a tax return is submitted on 31 March following the end of the tax year, the taxpayer would be subject to a penalty of £150.		
(e)	If a tax return is submitted on 31 May (approximately 14 months after the end of the tax year), the taxpayer would be subject to a penalty of £100 plus a daily penalty.		
(f)	Late payment of a final balancing payment of income tax by more than 30 days will be subject to a penalty of 5% of the tax due.		

5.3   Charlie is a higher rate taxpayer. He deliberately concealed the dividends that he received when he completed his tax return.

Select the correct statement from the following.   ✓

		True	False
(a)	Charlie did nothing wrong as the tax on dividends has already been deducted.		
(b)	Charlie did nothing wrong as dividends are exempt from income tax.		
(c)	Charlie will be subject to a penalty of between 30% and 100% of the dividend income that he has not declared.		
(d)	Charlie will be subject to a penalty of between 30% and 100% of the extra income tax that is due on the dividends.		
(e)	Charlie cannot be charged a penalty if it is his first offence.		

5.4   Wayne earns £45,000 per year from his job as a sales manager, and is entitled to a diesel company car and all fuel (business and private). The car has a list price of £22,000, but was purchased at a discount for £19,500. It has emissions of 159 g/km.

Wayne makes cash contributions of £1,600 per year into a personal pension scheme.

Calculate Wayne's tax liability (to the nearest £), using the following table.

Workings	
	£
Salary	
Car benefit	
Fuel Benefit	
Personal allowance	
Taxable income	
Tax at 20%:	
Tax at 40%	
Total tax liability	

5.5   Mike earns £45,000 per year from his job, and is entitled to a petrol company car and all fuel (business and private). The car has a list price of £16,000. It has emissions of 129 g/km.

Mike also received an interest free loan from his employer of £12,000 on 6 October in the tax year. He has not made any repayments.

Mike paid his own professional subscriptions of £200.

Assume that the official HMRC rate is 4.00%.

Complete supplementary page E1 of Mike's tax return as far as possible (see next page for the 2011/12 version).

5.6   Rachel had employment income of £91,500 and received dividends of £15,750. She paid £1,200 (net) into a personal pension scheme.

Calculate her total income tax liability (ie before deduction of tax paid) for the tax year, using the table given below.

	£
Employment Income	
Gross dividends	
Personal allowance	
Taxable income	

5.5 continued...

HM Revenue & Customs

Employment
Tax year 6 April 2011 to 5 April 2012

Your name

Your Unique Taxpayer Reference (UTR)

Complete an *Employment* page for each employment or directorship

1 Pay from this employment – the total from your P45 or P60 - *before tax was taken off*

£ · 0 0

2 UK tax taken off pay in box 1

£ · 0 0

3 Tips and other payments not on your P60 - *read page EN 4 of the notes*

£ · 0 0

4 PAYE tax reference of your employer (on your P45/P60)

/

5 Your employer's name

6 If you were a company director, put 'X' in the box

7 And, if the company was a close company, put 'X' in the box

8 If you are a part-time teacher in England or Wales and are on the Repayment of Teachers' Loans Scheme for this employment, put 'X' in the box

Benefits from your employment – use your form P11D (or equivalent information)

9 Company cars and vans – *the total 'cash equivalent' amount*

£ · 0 0

10 Fuel for company cars and vans - *the total 'cash equivalent' amount*

£ · 0 0

11 Private medical and dental insurance - *the total 'cash equivalent' amount*

£ · 0 0

12 Vouchers, credit cards and excess mileage allowance

£ · 0 0

13 Goods and other assets provided by your employer - *the total value or amount*

£ · 0 0

14 Accommodation provided by your employer - *the total value or amount*

£ · 0 0

15 Other benefits (including interest-free and low interest loans) - *the total 'cash equivalent' amount*

£ · 0 0

16 Expenses payments received and balancing charges

£ · 0 0

Employment expenses

17 Business travel and subsistence expenses

£ · 0 0

18 Fixed deductions for expenses

£ · 0 0

19 Professional fees and subscriptions

£ · 0 0

20 Other expenses and capital allowances

£ · 0 0

ⓘ **Shares schemes, employment lump sums, compensation, deductions and Seafarers' Earnings Deduction** are on the *Additional information* pages enclosed in the tax return pack

SA102 2012 · Tax return: Employment: Page E 1 · HMRC 12/11

6

Chapter activities

Capital gains tax – the main principles

6.1 For each statement, tick the appropriate box.

✓

		Actual Proceeds Used	Deemed proceeds used	No gain or loss basis
(a)	Father gives an asset to his son			
(b)	Wife sells an asset to her husband			
(c)	Simon gives an asset to his friend			
(d)	Margaret sells an asset to her cousin for £15,000 when the market value is £40,000			
(e)	Brian gives an asset to his civil partner, Dave.			

6.2 Alex bought an asset in January 2008 for £36,000, selling it in December 2012 for £35,000. He paid auctioneers commission of 4% when he bought the asset and 5% when he sold the asset.

The loss on this asset is:

✓

£nil	
£1,000	
£4,190	
£2,440	

True or false: legal fees are an allowable deduction where they relate to the purchase or sale of an asset.

6.3 State which of the following statements are true:

	True	False
(a) The annual exemption is applied after capital losses are deducted.		
(b) Capital losses from the same year cannot safeguard the annual exemption.		
(c) Capital gains are taxed at 28% for higher rate tax payers.		
(d) Capital losses can be set against gains of the previous tax year.		
(e) Capital losses brought forward can safeguard the annual exemption when offset against current year gains.		

6.4 Josie has a capital loss brought forward of £4,000. She is a higher rate income tax payer.

She sold an asset during the tax year for £19,000. She had been given the asset by her husband when it was worth £8,000. Her husband originally paid £6,500 for the asset.

Complete the following sentences:

(a) The gain on the asset is £ _____

(b) The amount of loss that will be relieved is £ _____

(c) The capital gains tax payable is £ _____

(d) The loss to be carried forward to the next tax year is £ _____

6.5 Complete the following table to show which assets are exempt from capital gains tax and which are chargeable.

Asset	Exempt	Chargeable
Antique furniture		
Principal private residence		
Clock		
Shares		
Holiday home		
Government securities		
Vintage car		
Land		

7 Chapter activities
Capital gains tax – some special rules

7.1 Richard bought a house on 1 January 2000 for £125,000. He lived in the house until 31 December 2002 when he moved abroad for one year to work. He returned from abroad on 31 December 2003, and then immediately moved into his elderly father's house until 30 June 2005, leaving his own home empty. He then moved back into his own house until 31 December 2010, when he moved to a new home and put the house on the market. The house was eventually sold on 1 January 2013 for £205,000.

(a) Which periods are treated as occupied and which are not?

Occupation / Deemed Occupation	Non-occupation

(b) What is the chargeable gain on the property?

£

7.2 The following table relates to sales of chattels.

Match the statements shown below to the correct asset details.

Asset	Sale proceeds	Cost	Statement
1	£4,000	£7,000	
2	£14,000	£8,000	
3	£8,000	£3,000	
4	£3,000	£5,000	
5	£15,000	£21,000	

Statements:

- ■ Exempt asset
- ■ Calculate gain as normal
- ■ Calculate loss as normal
- ■ Sale proceeds to be £6,000
- ■ Chattel marginal relief applies

7.3 Paul bought 20,000 shares in Lincoln Ltd for £5 per share in October 2000. He received a bonus issue of 1 for 25 shares in March 2003. In January 2013, Paul sold 8,000 shares for £9 per share.

Clearly showing the balance of shares, and their value, to carry forward, calculate the gain made on these shares. All workings must be shown in your calculations.

7.4   Bob sold the following assets in August 2012. These were his only disposals during the tax year.

Description	Sale Proceeds £	Cost £
Holiday home	230,000	150,000
Listed shares in B plc	20,000	35,000
Listed shares in C plc	18,000	10,000
Unlisted shares in D ltd	48,000	32,000

Use this information to complete pages CG1 and CG2 of Bob's tax return.

The 2011/12 version is shown on the next pages.

Capital gains summary
Tax year 6 April 2011 to 5 April 2012

1	Your name	2	Your Unique Taxpayer Reference (UTR)

Summary of your enclosed computations

Read the notes on pages CGN 10 to CGN 12 before completing this section.

You must enclose your computations, including details of each gain or loss, as well as filling in the boxes.

3 Total gains *(Boxes 19+25+31+32)*

£ · 0 0

4 Gains qualifying for Entrepreneurs' Relief (but excluding gains deferred from before 23 June 2010) - *read the notes on page CGN 11*

£ · 0 0

5 Box 5 is not in use

6 Total losses of the year - *enter '0' if there are none*

£ · 0 0

7 Losses brought forward and used in the year

£ · 0 0

8 Adjustment to Capital Gains Tax - *see notes*

£ · 0 0

9 Additional liability in respect of non-resident or dual resident trusts

£ · 0 0

10 Losses available to be carried forward to later years

£ · 0 0

11 Losses used against an earlier year's gain (special circumstances apply - *read the notes on page CGN 12*)

£ · 0 0

12 Losses used against income - *amount claimed against 2011-12 income*

£ · 0 0

13 Losses used against income - *amount claimed against 2010-11 income*

£ · 0 0

14 Income losses of 2011-12 set against gains

£ · 0 0

15 Deferred gains from before 23 June 2010 qualifying for Entrepreneurs' Relief

£ · 0 0

Listed shares and securities

16 Number of disposals - *read the notes on page CGN 14*

17 Disposal proceeds

£ · 0 0

18 Allowable costs (including purchase price)

£ · 0 0

19 Gains in the year, before losses

£ · 0 0

20 If you are making any claim or election, put 'X' in the box

21 If your computations include any estimates or valuations, put 'X' in the box

Unlisted shares and securities

| 22 | **Number of disposals** - *read the notes on page CGN 14* |

| 23 | **Disposal proceeds** |
£ . 0 0

| 24 | **Allowable costs (including purchase price)** |
£ . 0 0

| 25 | **Gains in the year, before losses** |
£ . 0 0

| 26 | **If you are making any claim or election, put 'X' in the box** |

| 27 | **If your computations include any estimates or valuations, put 'X' in the box** |

Property and other assets and gains

| 28 | **Number of disposals** |

| 29 | **Disposal proceeds** |
£ . 0 0

| 30 | **Allowable costs (including purchase price)** |
£ . 0 0

| 31 | **Gains in the year, before losses** |
£ . 0 0

| 32 | **Attributed gains where personal losses cannot be set off** |
£ . 0 0

| 33 | **Box 33 is not in use** |

| 34 | **If you are making any claim or election, put 'X' in the box** |

| 35 | **If your computations include any estimates or valuations, put 'X' in the box** |

Any other information

| 36 | **Please give any other information in this space** |

7.5   Jason disposed of three assets during the tax year as follows:

- An antique painting was sold for £12,100. It had been bought for £3,000.

- A quarter acre piece of land was sold for £10,000. It had been bought as part of a two-acre plot for £12,000. The remaining land was valued at £15,000 at the time of the sale.

- A holiday cottage was sold for £230,000. It had been bought for £195,000, and Jason had spent £38,000 extending it.

Jason is a higher rate income tax payer.

Complete the following sentences:

(a)   The gain on the painting is

£

(b)   The gain on the land is

£

(c)   The result of the sale of the holiday cottage is a gain / loss of

£

(d)   The capital gains tax payable is

£

Answers to chapter activities

Chapter activities

Introduction to income tax

1.1

		True	False
(a)	An individual's tax records only need to be kept until one year after the end of the tax year, unless an investigation is being carried out.		✓
(b)	It is not the taxpayer's responsibility to inform HMRC of any untaxed taxable income, unless they have been asked to complete a tax return.		✓
(c)	Accountants must normally follow the rules of confidentiality, but there are exceptions.	✓	
(d)	Where a practitioner has knowledge or suspicion that his client is money laundering, then he has a duty to inform the relevant person or authority.	✓	
(e)	Accountants should warn clients if they suspect money laundering to give the client a chance to cease the activity.		✓
(f)	When an accountant is advising a client the greatest duty of care is to the client.	✓	

1.2

		Yes	No
(a)	HMRC extra-statutory concessions	✓	
(b)	Statute law	✓	
(c)	HMRC statements of practice	✓	
(d)	Case law	✓	
(e)	Website www.hmrc.gov.uk	✓	
(f)	Website www.statistics.gov.uk		✓
(g)	HMRC guides and help sheets	✓	

1.3

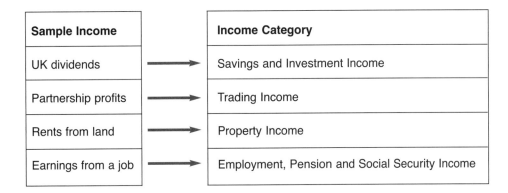

Sample Income		Income Category
UK dividends	→	Savings and Investment Income
Partnership profits	→	Trading Income
Rents from land	→	Property Income
Earnings from a job	→	Employment, Pension and Social Security Income

1.4

Income Category	Accruals Basis	Receipts Basis
Property Income	✓	
Savings and Investment Income		✓
Trading Income	✓	
Employment, Pension and Social Security Income		✓

1.5

Income Category	Exempt	Not Exempt
(a) Employment income		✓
(b) Income from an ISA	✓	
(c) Premium bond prizes	✓	
(d) Rent received from a buy-to-let property		✓
(e) Betting winnings (unless a professional gambler)	✓	
(f) Lottery prizes	✓	

Chapter activities
2 Income from property

2.1

	Two bedroom house	One bedroom flat
	£	£
Income	8,500	6,600
Expenses:		
Irrecoverable rent	850	
Management fees	765	
Redecoration	530	
Council Tax & Water		1,100
Insurance		340
Wear & Tear Allowance		550
Profit	6,355	4,610

2.2

		True	False
(a)	The maximum amount of gross rent that can be received tax free under the rent a room scheme is £5,250.		✓
(b)	The rent a room scheme only applies to furnished accommodation.	✓	
(c)	Rent a room relief can be claimed for guest houses provided it is also the claimant's main residence.	✓	
(d)	Taxpayers can claim both rent a room relief and wear and tear allowance for the same property.		✓
(e)	Eligible taxpayers do not have to claim rent a room relief if they choose not to.	✓	
(f)	Rent a room relief can only be claimed by owner-occupiers.		✓
(g)	Charges for goods or services like food or laundry are ignored when calculating the gross rent.		✓

2.3

		True	False
(a)	The rental of caravans qualifies as furnished holiday lettings	✓	
(b)	The rental of caravans is treated as a hobby and is exempt from tax		✓
(c)	Although the caravans are furnished, wear and tear allowance cannot be claimed as these are holiday lettings	✓	
(d)	Interest on loans to buy the caravans can be claimed as allowable expenses	✓	
(e)	Rent a room relief can be claimed against the rental income		✓

2.4   (i)

	Claiming rent a room relief	Normal rental income computation
	£	£
Income	10,920	10,920
Allowable deductions:		
Rent a room relief	4,250	
Heating		150
Food		780
Wear and Tear Allowance		1,092
Assessable amount	6,670	8,898

(ii) To pay the minimum income tax, Mahjabeen should **claim** rent a room relief.

2.5   (a)

	£	£
Income		12,000
Expenditure:		
Council tax	700	
Water rates	300	
Insurance	380	
Managing agent's charges	1,200	
Wear and tear (10% x [12,000 – 700 – 300])	1,100	
		3,680
Assessable Income		8,320

(b) Property income

Do not include furnished holiday lettings, Real Estate Investment Trust or Property Authorised Investment Funds dividends/distributions here.

20 Total rents and other income from property

£ 1 2 0 0 0 . 0 0

21 Tax taken off any income in box 20

£ . 0 0

22 Premiums for the grant of a lease – *from box E on the Working Sheet on page UKPN 8 of the notes.*

£ . 0 0

23 Reverse premiums and inducements

£ . 0 0

Property expenses

24 Rent, rates, insurance, ground rents etc.

£ 1 3 8 0 . 0 0

25 Property repairs, maintenance and renewals

£ . 0 0

26 Loan interest and other financial costs

£ . 0 0

27 Legal, management and other professional fees

£ 1 2 0 0 . 0 0

28 Costs of services provided, including wages

£ . 0 0

29 Other allowable property expenses

£ . 0 0

Calculating your taxable profit or loss

30 Private use adjustment – *read page UKPN 9 of the notes*

£ . 0 0

31 Balancing charges – *read page UKPN 10 of the notes*

£ . 0 0

32 Annual Investment Allowance

£ . 0 0

33 Business Premises Renovation Allowance (Assisted Areas only) – *read page UKPN 11 of the notes*

£ . 0 0

34 All other capital allowances

£ . 0 0

35 Landlord's Energy Saving Allowance

£ . 0 0

36 10% wear and tear allowance – *for furnished residential accommodation only*

£ 1 1 0 0 . 0 0

37 Rent a Room exempt amount

£ . 0 0

38 Adjusted profit for the year – *from box O on the Working Sheet on page UKPN 16*

£ 8 3 2 0 . 0 0

39 Loss brought forward used against this year's profits

£ . 0 0

40 Taxable profit for the year (box 38 minus box 39)

£ 8 3 2 0 . 0 0

41 Adjusted loss for the year – *from box O on the Working Sheet on page UKPN 16*

£ . 0 0

42 Loss set off against 2011-12 total income – *this will be unusual – read page UKPN 15 of the notes*

£ . 0 0

43 Loss to carry forward to following year, including unused losses brought forward

£ . 0 0

3 Chapter activities
Income from savings and investments

3.1

Received net	Received gross
Loan stock from quoted company	NS&I easy access savings account
Local authority loan	Treasury stock (a type of Gilt)
Online building society account	NS&I investment account

3.2 (i) (d) £100 (tax credit on dividends of £900 x 10/90 is treated as tax already paid)

(ii) (b) £1,480 (dividends plus tax credit £1,000 + gross interest £480)

3.3

(a) Government Stocks (Gilts)		
(b) UK Dividends		
(c) NS&I Index-linked Savings Certificates	✓	
(d) Building Society Cash ISA	✓	
(e) Bank ISA operated by post	✓	
(f) Local Authority Loans		

3.4

Total ISA limit	(e)	£11,280
Cash ISA limit	(c)	£5,640

3.5

Investment	Amount Received £	Assessable Amount £	Tax treated as paid £
Bank Account	560	700	140
UK Dividends	2,700	3,000	300
Cash ISA	120	0	0
NS&I fixed interest savings certificate	400	0	0
Debenture interest	800	1,000	200
Totals	4,580	4,700	640

<table>
<tr><td>**4**</td><td>**Chapter activities**
Income from employment</td></tr>
</table>

4.1

Indicators of Employment	Indicators of Self Employment
Need to do the work yourself	Can employ helper or substitute
Told how, where and when to do work	Decide yourself how, when and where to do work
Work set hours and paid regular wage with sick pay and holidays	Choose work hours and invoice for work done
No risk of capital or losses	Risk own capital and bear losses from work that is not to standard
Employer provides equipment	Provide own equipment
Usually work for one employer	Work for several people or organisations

4.2 **(1)** (a) 111 g/km   13%

(b) 134 g/km   17%

(c) 151 g/km   21%

(d) 249 g/km   35%

(2) (a) The cost of the car used in the benefit in kind computation is £17,000

(b) The percentage used in the benefit in kind computation is 27%

(c) The assessable benefit for Silvia relating to the car for 2012/13 is £2,295

4.3 **(1)** £75,000

(2)

		Yes	No
(a)	House provided for a vicar	✓	
(b)	House provided by employer for accountant working for a housing association		✓
(c)	Flat in sheltered accommodation provided for an on-site care manager	✓	

(3) £10,500   *(£9,300 + (4% x £90,000) - £2,400)*

4.4   £42   *(£6,000+£4,000)/2 x 4/12 x (4% – 1.5%)*

4.5   **(1)**   (b)   She will have a taxable amount of £875.

(10,000 x (50p – 45p)) + (1,500 x (50p – 25p))

(2)   (b)   His taxable salary will be reduced by £1,420.

(£28,400 x 5%, the employer's contribution is tax-free)

(3)   (b)   An allowable deduction of £120. (The net cost to Steve)

(4)   (a)   The employer pays a percentage of her salary into the scheme, but Genna does not.

5 Chapter activities
Preparing income tax computations

5.1

	£
Income	25,000
Gross dividends	1,350
	26,350
Personal allowance	10,435
Taxable income	15,915
Tax: general income	
14,565 x 20%	2,913
dividends	
1,350 x 10%	135
Tax liability	3,048

Personal allowance working:

Total Income	£26,350
Less grossed-up gift aid payments (£400 x 100/80)	£ 500
Income for comparison with limit	£25,850

His age-related allowance would be calculated as follows:

Age-related allowance – aged 75 and over	£10,660
Less restriction 50% x (£25,850 – £25,400)	£ 225
Allowance	£10,435

5.2

		True	False
(a)	Payments on account relating to a tax year are paid on 31 January in the tax year, and on 31 July following the tax year.	✓	
(b)	The final payment of income tax relating to a tax year is paid on 31 October following the end of the tax year.		✓
(c)	If a taxpayer is late paying income tax then he will either be subject to a penalty or interest, but not both.		✓
(d)	If a tax return is submitted on 31 March following the end of the tax year, the taxpayer would be subject to a penalty of £150.		✓
(e)	If a tax return is submitted on 31 May (approximately 14 months after the end of the tax year), the taxpayer would be subject to a penalty of £100 plus a daily penalty.	✓	
(f)	Late payment of a final balancing payment of income tax by more than 30 days will be subject to a penalty of 5% of the tax due.	✓	

5.3

		True	False
(a)	Charlie did nothing wrong as the tax on dividends has already been deducted.		✓
(b)	Charlie did nothing wrong as dividends are exempt from income tax.		✓
(c)	Charlie will be subject to a penalty of between 30% and 100% of the dividend income that he has not declared.		✓
(d)	Charlie will be subject to a penalty of between 30% and 100% of the extra income tax that is due on the dividends.	✓	
(e)	Charlie cannot be charged a penalty if it is his first offence.		✓

5.4

Workings	
	£
Salary	45,000
Car benefit £22,000 x (11% + 11% + 3%)	5,500
Fuel Benefit £20,200 x 25%	5,050
Sub total	55,550
Personal allowance	8,105
Taxable income	47,445
Tax at 20%: Band £34,370 + (1,600 x 100/80) = 36,370 x 20%	7,274
Tax at 40% (£47,445 − £36,370) x 40%	4,430
Total tax liability	11,704

5.5

HM Revenue & Customs

Employment
Tax year 6 April 2011 to 5 April 2012

Your name

Mike

Your Unique Taxpayer Reference (UTR)

Complete an *Employment* page for each employment or directorship

1 Pay from this employment – the total from your P45 or P60 – *before tax was taken off*

£ 4 5 0 0 0 . 0 0

2 UK tax taken off pay in box 1

£ . 0 0

3 Tips and other payments not on your P60
 – *read page EN 4 of the notes*

£ . 0 0

4 PAYE tax reference of your employer (on your P45/P60)

/

5 Your employer's name

6 If you were a company director, put 'X' in the box

7 And, if the company was a close company, put 'X' in the box

8 If you are a part-time teacher in England or Wales and are on the Repayment of Teachers' Loans Scheme for this employment, put 'X' in the box

Benefits from your employment – use your form P11D (or equivalent information)

9 Company cars and vans – *the total 'cash equivalent' amount*

£ 2 5 6 0 . 0 0

10 Fuel for company cars and vans – *the total 'cash equivalent' amount*

£ 3 2 3 2 . 0 0

11 Private medical and dental insurance – *the total 'cash equivalent' amount*

£ . 0 0

12 Vouchers, credit cards and excess mileage allowance

£ . 0 0

13 Goods and other assets provided by your employer – *the total value or amount*

£ . 0 0

14 Accommodation provided by your employer – *the total value or amount*

£ . 0 0

15 Other benefits (including interest-free and low interest loans) – *the total 'cash equivalent' amount*

£ 2 4 0 . 0 0

16 Expenses payments received and balancing charges

£ . 0 0

Employment expenses

17 Business travel and subsistence expenses

£ . 0 0

18 Fixed deductions for expenses

£ . 0 0

19 Professional fees and subscriptions

£ 2 0 0 . 0 0

20 Other expenses and capital allowances

£ . 0 0

ⓘ **Shares schemes, employment lump sums, compensation, deductions and Seafarers' Earnings Deduction** are on the *Additional information* pages enclosed in the tax return pack

5.6

	£
Employment Income	91,500
Gross dividends	17,500
	109,000
Personal allowance	4,355
Taxable income	104,645
General income:	
(34,370 + 1,500) x 20%	7,174
(87,145* − 35,870) x 40%	20,510
Dividend income	
17,500 x 32.5%	5,687
Tax liability	33,371

Workings:

Adjusted net income: £91,500 + £17,500 - £1,500 = £107,500

Personal alllowance: £8,105 − 50% x (£107,500 − £100,000) = £4,355

* General income: £91,500 − £4,355 = £87,145

6 Chapter activities
Capital gains tax – the main principles

6.1

	Actual Proceeds Used	Deemed proceeds used	No gain or loss basis
(a) Father gives an asset to his son		✓	
(b) Wife sells an asset to her husband			✓
(c) Simon gives an asset to his friend		✓	
(d) Margaret sells an asset to her cousin for £15,000 when the market value is £40,000	✓		
(e) Brian gives an asset to his civil partner, Dave.			✓

6.2   £4,190

True: legal fees are an allowable deduction where they relate to the purchase or sale of an asset.

6.3

	True	False
(a) The annual exemption is applied after capital losses are deducted.	✓	
(b) Capital losses from the same year cannot safeguard the annual exemption.	✓	
(c) Capital gains are taxed at 28% for higher rate tax payers.	✓	
(d) Capital losses can be set against gains of the previous tax year.		✓
(e) Capital losses brought forward can safeguard the annual exemption when offset against current year gains.	✓	

6.4   (a)   The gain on the asset is £12,500

(b)   The amount of loss that will be relieved is £1,900

(c)   The capital gains tax payable is £0

(d)   The loss to be carried forward to the next tax year is £2,100

6.5

Asset	Exempt	Chargeable
Antique furniture		✓
Principal private residence	✓	
Clock	✓	
Shares		✓
Holiday home		✓
Government securities	✓	
Vintage car	✓	
Land		✓

7 Chapter activities
Capital gains tax – some special rules

7.1 **(a)**

Occupation / Deemed Occupation	Non-occupation
1/1/2000 - 31/12/2002 (36 months)	
1/1/2003 - 31/12/2003 (12 months)	
1/1/2004 - 30/6/2005 (18 months)	
1/7/2005 - 31/12/2010 (66 months)	
1/1/2011 - 1/1/2013 (24 months)	

(b) Chargeable gain is £nil (all periods are occupation or deemed occupation)

7.2

Asset	Sale proceeds	Cost	Statement
1	£4,000	£7,000	Sale proceeds to be £6,000
2	£14,000	£8,000	Calculate gain as normal
3	£8,000	£3,000	Chattel marginal relief applies
4	£3,000	£5,000	Exempt asset
5	£15,000	£21,000	Calculate loss as normal

7.3

	Number of shares	£
October 2000	20,000	100,000
Bonus	800	0
Sub total	20,800	100,000
Disposal	8,000	38,462
Pool balance	12,800	61,538
Proceeds		72,000
Cost		38,462
Gain		33,538

7.4

HM Revenue & Customs

Capital gains summary
Tax year 6 April 2011 to 5 April 2012

1	Your name
	B O B

2	Your Unique Taxpayer Reference (UTR)

Summary of your enclosed computations

Read the notes on pages CGN 10 to CGN 12 before completing this section.

You must enclose your computations, including details of each gain or loss, as well as filling in the boxes.

3	Total gains *(Boxes 19+25+31+32)*
	£ 1 0 4 0 0 0 . 0 0

4	Gains qualifying for Entrepreneurs' Relief (but excluding gains deferred from before 23 June 2010) - *read the notes on page CGN 11*
	£ . 0 0

5 Box 5 is not in use

6	Total losses of the year - *enter '0' if there are none*
	£ 1 5 0 0 0 . 0 0

7	Losses brought forward and used in the year
	£ . 0 0

8	Adjustment to Capital Gains Tax - *see notes*
	£ . 0 0

9	Additional liability in respect of non-resident or dual resident trusts
	£ . 0 0

10	Losses available to be carried forward to later years
	£ . 0 0

11	Losses used against an earlier year's gain (special circumstances apply - *read the notes on page CGN 12*)
	£ . 0 0

12	Losses used against income - *amount claimed against 2011-12 income*
	£ . 0 0

13	Losses used against income - *amount claimed against 2010-11 income*
	£ . 0 0

14	Income losses of 2011-12 set against gains
	£ . 0 0

15	Deferred gains from before 23 June 2010 qualifying for Entrepreneurs' Relief
	£ . 0 0

Listed shares and securities

16	Number of disposals - *read the notes on page CGN 14*
	2

17	Disposal proceeds
	£ 3 8 0 0 0 . 0 0

18	Allowable costs (including purchase price)
	£ 4 5 0 0 0 . 0 0

19	Gains in the year, before losses
	£ 8 0 0 0 . 0 0

20	If you are making any claim or election, put 'X' in the box

21	If your computations include any estimates or valuations, put 'X' in the box

Unlisted shares and securities

22 Number of disposals - *read the notes on page CGN 14*

`1`

23 Disposal proceeds

£ `4 8 0 0 0 · 0 0`

24 Allowable costs (including purchase price)

£ `3 2 0 0 0 · 0 0`

25 Gains in the year, before losses

£ `1 6 0 0 0 · 0 0`

26 If you are making any claim or election, put 'X' in the box

27 If your computations include any estimates or valuations, put 'X' in the box

Property and other assets and gains

28 Number of disposals

`1`

29 Disposal proceeds

£ `2 3 0 0 0 0 · 0 0`

30 Allowable costs (including purchase price)

£ `1 5 0 0 0 0 · 0 0`

31 Gains in the year, before losses

£ `· 0 0`

32 Attributed gains where personal losses cannot be set off

£ `8 0 0 0 0 · 0 0`

33 Box 33 is not in use

34 If you are making any claim or election, put 'X' in the box

35 If your computations include any estimates or valuations, put 'X' in the box

Any other information

36 Please give any other information in this space

7.5 (a) The gain on the painting is £9,100

(b) The gain on the land is £5,200

(c) The result of the sale of the holiday cottage is a **loss** of £3,000

(d) The capital gains tax payable is £196

Personal taxation

Practice assessment 1

Section 1

Task 1.1

State whether each of the following statements is true or false.   ✓

		True	False
(a)	An individual's tax records all need to be kept until five years after the end of the tax year, unless an investigation is being carried out.		✓
(b)	It is the taxpayer's responsibility to inform HMRC of any untaxed taxable income that HMRC are not aware of.	✓	

Task 1.2

State whether each of the following statements is true or false.

✓

		True	False
(a)	Accountants must always follow the rules of confidentiality. There are no exceptions.		✓
(b)	Where a practitioner has knowledge that his client is money laundering, then he should resign from acting for the client, but take no other action.		✓
(c)	Accountants should never warn clients if they suspect that they are money laundering and are about to report them.	✓	
(d)	When an accountant is advising a client the greatest duty of care is to the accountant's professional body.		✓
(e)	HMRC has powers to visit premises to inspect records.	✓	
(f)	HMRC has no duty to act in any particular way with regard to their compliance checks.		✓

Task 1.3

Select from the following list, those that indicate employment.

		✓
(a)	The contract is a contract of service	✓
(b)	Choose work hours and invoice for work done	
(c)	Told how, where and when to do work	✓
(d)	No risk of capital	✓
(e)	Decide yourself how, when and where to do work	
(f)	Can employ helper or substitute	
(g)	Equipment is provided	✓
(h)	Bear losses from work that is not to standard	
(i)	Work set hours and paid regular wage with sick pay and holidays	✓
(j)	Usually work for one employer	✓
(k)	Provide own equipment	

Task 1.4

Jenny has provided you with the following information regarding her employment.

She is paid monthly. Her annual salary was £21,600 for the year ended 31 August 2012, and *5 months 9000* £22,800 for the year ended 31 August 2013.

7 months 13300 She received a bonus of £1,200 on 15 October 2012. This related to the year ended 31 August 2012. She received a bonus of £1,800 on 20 October 2013. This related to the year ended 31 August 2013.

The company paid a pension contribution of 6% of her total employment pay into the company pension scheme.

Complete the following with respect to the tax year 2012/13.

The taxable salary (excluding bonus) is £ *22300*

The taxable bonus is £ *1200*

The company contribution to the pension scheme is £ *1338*

The total assessable employment income for Jenny is £ *23500*

Task 1.5

(1) What scale charge precentage would be applied for petrol cars with the following CO_2 emissions?

(a) 99 g/km *10%*
(b) 140 g/km *19%*
(c) 171 g/km *25%*
(d) 241 g/km *35%*

(2) Steve was provided with a second hand company car on 6 November 2012. *5 months.* It cost the company £9,000, but the list price of this car when bought new was £16,000. The car has a CO_2 emission of 151g/km, and has a diesel engine. The company pays for all running costs, except private fuel.

(a) The cost of the car used in the benefit in kind computation is £ *16000*

(b) The percentage used in the benefit in kind computation is *24* %

(c) The assessable benefit for Steve relating to the car for 2012/13 is £ *1600*

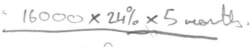

16000 × 24% × 5 months.

12

Task 1.6

(1) When accommodation is purchased by an employer, what is the value of the property above which an additional benefit is applied?

✓

(a)	£50,000	
(b)	£75,000	✓
(c)	£100,000	
(d)	£125,000	
(e)	£150,000	

(2) Would the following situations be treated as being job-related where no accommodation benefit arises?

✓

		Yes	No
(a)	House provided for a finance director		✓
(b)	House provided by employer for librarian working for local authority		✓
(c)	Flat in nursing home provided for an on-site nursing manager	✓	

(3) Sian was provided with accommodation in the form of a flat that the employer purchased for £125,000. It is not job related. The flat has an annual value £6,300. The employer also bought furniture for the flat, costing £2,000. Assume that the HMRC official interest rate is 4.00%. Her taxable benefit is:

✓

(a)	£6,300	
(b)	£8,300	
(c)	£8,700	✓
(d)	£9,700	
(e)	£10,300	

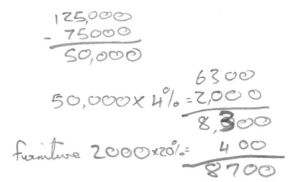

Task 1.7

Using the following table, analyse the benefits into those that are exempt from tax, and those that are taxable.

✓

Description	Exempt	Taxable
Interest-free loans not exceeding £5,000	✓	
Cash payment to employee to help with childcare costs		✓
Employer contributions to company pension scheme	✓	
Free meals in a staff restaurant only available to senior managers		✓
Performance related bonus payment		✓
Provision of one mobile telephone and its running costs	✓	
Holiday pay		✓
Use of a bicycle and helmet to commute to work	✓	
Childcare vouchers up to £55 per week for basic rate taxpayers	✓	

Task 1.8

(1) Davina uses her own car for business travelling. During the tax year she travelled 12,500 business miles for which she was paid 45p per mile by her employer. The impact of this is:

5 6 25
5 1 25
500

	✓
(a) She will have a taxable amount of £500.	✓
(b) She will have a taxable amount of £5,625.	
(c) She will have a taxable amount of zero.	
(d) She will claim an allowable expense of £500.	

12500 × 0·45 = 5625

10000 × 0·45 = 4500
2500 × 0·25 = 625
5125

5625 - 5125 = 500

(2) Elisa has an occupational pension scheme to which she contributes 6% of her salary. Her employer contributes 8% of her salary. Her salary is £39,400. The impact of this is:

↳ Disregard this.

	✓
(a) Her taxable salary will be increased by £3,152.	
(b) Her taxable salary will be reduced by £2,364.	✓
(c) Her taxable salary will be increased by £788.	
(d) Her basic rate band will be extended by £2,955.	

(3) Stephan pays £320 per year in subscriptions to professional bodies. His employer gave him an allowance of £400 to cover professional subscriptions. The impact of this is:

	✓
(a) No impact on tax.	
(b) An allowable deduction of £320.	
(c) A taxable amount of £80.	✓
(d) A taxable amount of £400.	

(4) Geraldine has a personal pension scheme, paying £200 each month by direct debit. The tax implications are:

	✓
(a) Geraldine's assessable employment income is reduced by £2,400 per year.	
(b) Geraldine's assessable employment income is reduced by £3,000 per year.	
(c) There are no tax implications.	
(d) Geraldine's basic rate band is extended by £3,000.	✓

200 × 12 = 2400

$$\frac{2400 \times 100}{80} = 3000$$

Task 1.9

Kerry has received the amounts shown on the following table from various investments. Complete the table to show the assessable amounts and the amounts of tax that are treated as having been paid.

Investment	Amount Received £	Assessable Amount £	Tax treated as paid £	
Building Society Account	1,500	1875 _{1500×100/80}	375	←-20%
Dividends from UK Cos.	4,950	5500 _{4950×100/90}	550	←-10%
Stocks & Shares ISA	190	—	—	
NS&I investment account	400	400	—	
Local authority loan interest	1,600	2000 _{1600×100/80}	400	←-20%
Totals	8,640	9775	1325	

Task 1.10

State which of the following sources provide tax-free (exempt) income:

	✓
(a) Government Stocks (Gilts)	
(b) NS&I Easy Access Account	
(c) NS&I Index-linked Savings Certificates	✓
(d) NS&I Fixed Interest Savings Certificates	✓
(e) Cash ISA	✓
(f) Unquoted company loans	

Task 1.11

Complete the following table to show the maximum investment in an ISA that an individual can make in 2012/13.

Total ISA limit	11280
Cash ISA limit	11280÷2 = 5640

Task 1.12

James, who is 77 years old, had pension income of £102,000 and received bank interest of £600 (net).

He paid £800 (net) to charities under the gift aid scheme.

Calculate his total income tax liability (ie before deduction of tax paid) for the tax year, using the table given below.

	£
Pension Income	102,000
Bank Interest GROSS $\frac{600 \times 100}{80}$	750
	102750
Personal Allowance	(7230)
Taxable Income	95520
Tax	
General: 34370 +1600×20%	7074
94770 - 35370×40%	23760
Saving 750×40%	300
Tax liability .	31134

102750 - 1000 = 101750
101750 - 100,000 = 1750
1750 × 50% = 875
8105 - 875 = 7230

Task 1.13

The company that you work for is changing from paying mileage allowances for staff using their own cars to providing pool cars for business travel.

Until now the company has paid 50p per mile for all business journeys in employees' own cars. Under the new system, pool cars will be available at the workplace for employees to use for business journeys only. Staff will need to fill up the car that they are using with petrol when necessary, and submit a claim for reimbursement from the company. All staff have already been told about the new system, but are not aware of any tax implications.

Required:

Write an email to all staff to compare the tax implications of the new scheme for staff with the previous scheme.

email
from:
to:
subject:
date:

Task 1.14

Simon rents out one furnished property. He claims wear and tear allowance. The following is a statement compiled from his accounting records relating to the tax year.

	£	£
Rental Income Receivable		10,000
less expenditure:		
Council Tax	720	
Water Rates	260	
Insurance	280	
Cost of replacement carpets	2,100 X	
Depreciation of Furniture	900 X	
Managing Agent's Charges	800	
		5,060
Profit		4,940

Required

(a)   Calculate the assessable property income for Simon, using the following table.

	£	£
Income		10,000
Expenditure:		
Council Tax	720	
Water Rates	260	
Insurance	280	
Managing Agent Charges.	800	
Wear & Tear 10,000 – 720 – 260 = 9020 9020 x 10% = 902	902	
		2962
Assessable Income		7038

(b)   Complete page UKP2 of the UK Property supplementary pages, (the 2011/12 version is reproduced on the next page) for Simon.

Property income

Do not include furnished holiday lettings, Real Estate Investment Trust or Property Authorised Investment Funds dividends/distributions here.

20 Total rents and other income from property

£ 1 0 0 0 0 . 0 0

21 Tax taken off any income in box 20

£ . 0 0

22 Premiums for the grant of a lease - *from box E on the Working Sheet on page UKPN 8 of the notes.*

£ . 0 0

23 Reverse premiums and inducements

£ . 0 0

Property expenses

24 Rent, rates, insurance, ground rents etc.

£ 1 2 6 0 . 0 0

25 Property repairs, maintenance and renewals

£ . 0 0

26 Loan interest and other financial costs

£ . 0 0

27 Legal, management and other professional fees

£ 8 0 0 . 0 0

28 Costs of services provided, including wages

£ . 0 0

29 Other allowable property expenses

£ . 0 0

Calculating your taxable profit or loss

30 Private use adjustment - *read page UKPN 9 of the notes*

£ . 0 0

31 Balancing charges - *read page UKPN 10 of the notes*

£ . 0 0

32 Annual Investment Allowance

£ . 0 0

33 Business Premises Renovation Allowance (Assisted Areas only) - *read page UKPN 11 of the notes*

£ . 0 0

34 All other capital allowances

£ . 0 0

35 Landlord's Energy Saving Allowance

£ . 0 0

36 10% wear and tear allowance - *for furnished residential accommodation only*

£ 9 0 2 . 0 0

37 Rent a Room exempt amount

£ . 0 0

38 Adjusted profit for the year - *from box O on the Working Sheet on page UKPN 16*

£ 7 0 3 8 . 0 0

39 Loss brought forward used against this year's profits

£ . 0 0

40 Taxable profit for the year (box 38 minus box 39)

£ 7 0 3 8 . 0 0

41 Adjusted loss for the year - *from box O on the Working Sheet on page UKPN 16*

£ . 0 0

42 Loss set off against 2011-12 total income - *this will be unusual - read page UKPN 15 of the notes*

£ . 0 0

43 Loss to carry forward to following year, including unused losses brought forward

£ . 0 0

Section 2

Task 2.1

Select the statements that are true from the following: ✓

		True	False
(a)	The maximum amount of gross rent that can be received tax free under the rent a room scheme is £4,250.	✓	
(b)	The rent a room scheme applies to both furnished and unfurnished accommodation.		✓
(c)	Taxpayers cannot claim both rent a room relief and wear and tear allowance for the same property.	✓	
(d)	Taxpayers must claim rent a room relief if they are eligible.		✓
(e)	Rent a room relief can only be claimed by owner-occupiers.		✓

Task 2.2

Charlie has two properties in addition to his home, details of which are as follows:

Two bedroom house:

(1)   This unfurnished house is rented out for £850 per month. The property was occupied this tax year until 31 January when the tenants moved out, with the rent paid up to date. The property was let again from 1 March at a rent of £900 per month.

(2)   Charlie paid £1510 for redecoration and repainting in February. He also spent £1,200 adding a porch to the house.

(3)   The only other expense paid by Charlie on the house was 12% management charge to the agent on rent received.

One bedroom flat:

(1)   This furnished flat is rented out for £490 per month. The property was rented all tax year.

(2)   Charlie paid council tax and water rates on the flat, totalling £1,160 for the period that the flat was occupied. He also paid buildings and contents insurance of £370 for the year.

Calculate the profit or loss made on each property, using the following table.

	Two bedroom house £	One bedroom flat £
Income	850×10=8500 +900 9400	490×12= 5880
Expenses:		
Rederoration & Repaint	(1510)	
Agent fees.	(1128)	
Council Tax & Water Rates		(1160)
Wear & Tear.		(588)
Insurance.		(370)
Profit.	6762	3762

Task 2.3

Mike rents a furnished room in his own house to a lodger for £260 per week, including breakfast and an evening meal. Heating the room costs Mike £170 for the year, and food for the lodger's meals costs £28 per week.

(1)   Calculate the assessable amount for the tax year, based on

    (a)   claiming rent a room relief, and

    (b)   preparing a normal rental income computation

    using the following table.

	Claiming rent a room relief £	Normal rental income computation £
Income	13,520	13,520
Allowable deductions		
Heating		170
Food		1456
Rent a Room Relief Allowance	4250	
Wear & Tear.		1352
Assessable Income	9270	10542

7416

(2)   Complete the following sentence:

To pay the minimum income tax, Mike should (**claim**)/ ~~not claim~~ rent a room relief.

Task 2.4

For each statement, tick the appropriate box.

✓

	Actual Proceeds Used	Deemed proceeds used	No gain or loss basis
(1) Dave gives an asset to his father		✓	
(2) Peter sells an asset to his friend	✓		
(3) Simon gives an asset to his friend		✓	

Task 2.5

John has a capital loss brought forward of £2,500. He has taxable income for the year of £25,000.

He sold an asset during the tax year for £21,000. He had been left the asset when his grandfather died. His grandfather had paid £6,000 for the asset, and it was valued at £9,500 at the time of death.

Complete the following sentences:

Limit of capital gain tax is 10600

(a)   The gain on the asset is   £ 11 500

(b)   The amount of loss that will be relieved is   £ 900   11500
                                                              -10600
                                                                 900

(c)   The capital gains tax payable is   £ 0

(d)   The loss to be carried forward to the next tax year is   £ 1600   2500
                                                                           900
                                                                          1600

25000

21,000

6000

Task 2.6

Pam bought 25,000 shares in Lester Ltd for £5 per share in October 2000. In April 2005 she took up a rights issue of 3 for 5 at £4 per share. In January 2013, Pam sold 10,000 shares for £8 per share.

Clearly showing the balance of shares, and their value, to carry forward calculate the gain made on these shares. All workings must be shown in your calculations.

		£
Oct 2000	25000×5 =	125000
April 2005 Rights Issue	$\frac{25000 \times 3}{5}$ = 15000 × 4	60000
	40000 ÷ →	185,000
	(10000) ←×	(46250)
Bal c/f	30,000	138750
Sold.	10,000×8	80000
Cost	10000	(46250)
		33750

Task 2.7

Complete the following table to show which assets are exempt from capital gains tax and which are chargeable.

Asset	Exempt	Chargeable
Land		✓
Principal private residence	✓	
Antique painting		✓
Unquoted shares		✓
Caravan	✓	
Government securities	✓	
Classic car	✓	
Horse	✓	

Task 2.8

Roger bought a house on 1 January 1999. He lived in the house until 31 December 2002 when he moved to Aberdeen to take up a job, where he stayed until 30 June 2006, while renting out his own house. He then moved back into his own house from 1 July 2006 until 31 December 2010, when he moved to a new home and put the house on the market. The house was eventually sold on 1 March 2013.

Which periods are treated as occupied and which are not?

Occupation / Deemed Occupation	Non-occupation
1/1/1999 – 31/12/2002 31/12/2002 - 30/6/2006 1/7/2006 – 31/12/2010 31/12/2010 – 1/3/2013	

Task 2.9

State which of the following statements are true and which are false: ✓

		True	False
(a)	The annual exemption is applied before current year capital losses are deducted, but after brought forward capital losses.		✓
(b)	Capital losses brought forward cannot safeguard the annual exemption.		✓
(c)	Capital gains are taxed at 18% for all taxpayers.		✓
(d)	Capital losses can be set against income of the previous tax year.		✓

Personal taxation

Practice assessment 2

This Assessment is based on a sample assessment provided by the AAT and is reproduced here with their kind permission.

Section 1

Task 1.1

Which of the following statements is true or false?

✓

	True	False
HMRC sends a tax return to every individual.		✓
All tax records should be kept for at least 6 years by an individual.		✓

Task 1.2

(1) Which of the following statements is not correct?

✓

(a)	Accountants need to follow the rules of confidentiality even in a social environment.	
(b)	Accountants are allowed to break the rules of confidentiality when money laundering is suspected.	
(c)	The rules of confidentiality need to be followed after the relationship in question has ended.	✓
(d)	Accountants must follow the rules of confidentiality, irrespective of the situation.	✓

(2) When an accountant is advising a client, to whom does he owe the greatest duty of care?

✓

(a)	HMRC	
(b)	The professional body to which the accountant belongs	
(c)	The client	✓
(d)	The public	

Task 1.3

For each statement, tick either employment or self-employment

✓

	Employment	Self Employment
Contract of service is for:	✓	
Contract for service is for:		✓
A high level of control by an employer over the work performed would indicate what type of relationship?	✓	

Task 1.4

Joanne provides you with the following information: 3 months – 4350

■ Her annual salary for the twelve months to 30 June 2012 was £17,400.
  9 months – 14580
■ Her annual salary for the twelve months to 30 June 2013 was £19,440

■ She received a bonus of £876 on 14 April 2012 based on the company's accounting profit for the year ended 31 March 2012.

■ She received a bonus of £960 on 17 April 2013 based on the company's accounting profit for the year ended 31 March 2013.

■ She receives a 5% commission in each tax year on her salary for that tax year.

Using this information:

(a) What is the salary taxable for 2012/13?   £ 18930

[options: £17,400; £19,440; £18,930; £18,420; £18,760]

(b) What is the bonus taxable for 2012/13?   £ 876

[options: £876; £960; £939; £918; £932]

(c) What is the commission for 2012/13?   £ 946.50

[options: £870; £972; £946.50; £921; £938]

Task 1.5

(1) What scale charge percentage would be applied for petrol cars with the following CO_2 emissions?

    (a) 112 g/km — 13%

    (b) 130 g/km — 17%

    (c) 145 g/km — 20%

    (d) 240 g/km — 35%

(2) Simon was provided with a second hand car in October 2010. *7 months* It cost the company £14,000, but the list price of this car when bought new was £21,000. The car has a CO_2 emission of 181g/km, and has a diesel engine. The company pays for all running costs, including business fuel.

    (a) The cost of the car used in the benefit in kind computation is   £21000

    (b) The emissions % used in the benefit in kind computation is   30 %

    (c) The benefit in kind for use of the car is   £ 6300 ?

    21000 × 30%

Task 1.6

(1) *9 months* On 6 July 2012, Ken was provided with a company loan of £20,000 on which he pays interest at 3% per annum. The official rate of interest is 4.00%.

What is the benefit in kind for 2012/13?

✓

(a)	£800	
(b)	£150	✓
(c)	£112	
(d)	£600	

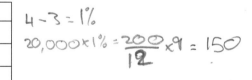

4 − 3 = 1%

$20,000 \times 1\% = \dfrac{200}{12} \times 9 = 150$

(2) When accommodation is purchased by an employer, what is the value of the property above which an additional benefit is applied?

✓

(a)	£50,000	
(b)	£70,000	
(c)	£75,000	✓
(d)	£100,000	

(3)   Would the following situations be treated as being job-related where no accommodation benefit arises?

✓

	Yes	No
(a) Accommodation provided for a caretaker of a school	✓	
(b) Accommodation provided for security reasons	✓	
(c) Accommodation provided for all directors		✓

(4)   Ethel was provided with accommodation (which is not job related) by her employer. The flat has an annual value £4,200 and the employer pays a rent of £300 per month. She pays £100 per month towards the private use of the flat. Her taxable benefit for 2012/13 is:

✓

(a)	£3,000	
(b)	£2,400	
(c)	£6,600	
(d)	£4,200	
(e)	£3,600	

(5)   Which two of the following statements are correct?

✓

(a)	Furniture provided by an employer is taxed at 20% per annum of the market value.	✓
(b)	Furniture provided by an employer is taxed on the cost to the employer in the year of purchase.	
(c)	Expenses paid for by the employer is taxed at 20% per annum of the cost.	
(d)	Expenses paid for by the employer are taxed on the cost to the employer.	✓

Task 1.7

Complete the following sentences so that the benefit is exempt from tax.

(1) Childcare vouchers provided by employers are exempt for basic rate tax payers up to the

first | £ 55 | per week.

(2) Provision of mobile telephones is restricted to | 1 | per employee.

(3) Long service awards are restricted to | £ 50 | value per year of service.

(4) Relocation expenses up to | £ 8000 | are allowed.

Options:

(1) £45; £50; £55; £60; £65

(2) 1; 2; 3

(3) £25; £50; £75; £100

(4) £5,000; £6,000; £8,000; £10,000

Task 1.8

(1)   Barrie uses his own car for business travelling. During the tax year, he travelled 16,000 business miles for which he was paid 35p per mile by his employer. The impact of this is:

	✓
(a) He will have a taxable amount of £1,600.	
(b) He will have a taxable amount of £400.	
(c) He will claim an allowable expense of £1,600.	
(d) He will claim an allowable expense of £400.	✓

$16000 \times 0.35 = 5600$
$10000 \times 0.45 = 4500$
$6000 \times 0.25 = \underline{1500}$
6000
$6000 - 5600 = 400$

(2)   Edward has an occupational pension scheme to which he contributes 4% of his salary. His employer also contributes 6% of his salary. His salary was £22,400. The impact of this is:

	✓
(a) His salary will be reduced by £896.	✓
(b) His salary will be reduced by £2,240.	
(c) His basic rate will be extended by £896.	
(d) His basic rate will be extended by £2,240.	

(3)   Simon pays £300 per year in subscriptions. £180 is paid to a professional body that he belongs to and the other £120 is paid to a social club where he regularly entertains clients. The impact of this is:

	✓
(a) Neither is allowable as a tax deduction.	
(b) Both are allowable as a tax deduction.	
(c) Only the professional fees are allowable.	✓
(d) Only the social club fees are allowable.	

(4)   George has a non-contributory occupational pension scheme. This means

	✓
(a) The employer pays a percentage of his salary into the scheme, but George does not.	✓
(b) George pays a percentage of his salary into the scheme, but the employer does not.	
(c) Only the Government pays a percentage of his salary into the scheme.	
(d) The employer and the Government pay a percentage of his salary into the scheme.	
(e) George and the Government pay a percentage of his salary into the scheme.	

Task 1.9

(1) Place the following types of investment income in the correct column:

List:

■ Interest from bank accounts

■ Interest from building society accounts

■ Interest from NS&I investment accounts

■ Gilts

■ NS&I income bonds

■ Loan stock from unquoted companies

Received net	Received gross
Interest from bank accs.	*Interest from NS&I investment accs.*
Interest from building Society accs	*Gilts*
Loan Stock from unquoted companies	*NS &I Income Bonds.*

(2) During the tax year, Harriet received interest of £320 from her building society account and £480 from her NS&I investment account. The tax treated as already paid on this interest totals:

		✓
(a)	£80	✓
(b)	£200	
(c)	£120	
(d)	£184	

$$\frac{320 \times 100}{80} = 400$$
$$(320)$$
$$80.$$

Task 1.10

(a) Victoria receives dividends of £216.

The tax on these dividends is   £   24

$$\frac{216 \times 100}{90} = 240$$
$$(216)$$
$$\overline{24}$$

[options: £21.60; £43.20; £54; £24]

(b) The gross amount of the dividend is   £   240

[options: £162; £192; £270; £240; £237.60; £259.20]

Task 1.11

(a) Complete the following sentence:

The maximum total that can be invested by an individual in an ISA for 2012/13 is

£ 11280

(b) Irrespective of the amount of money involved, lottery winnings are exempt from tax.

True /False

Task 1.12 £10,500

Roger, who is 67 years old, had income of £27,000 and received dividends of £936.

Calculate his total income tax liability for the tax year, using the table given below.

	£
Income	27,000
Gross Dividends	1040
	28,040
Personal Allowance	(9180)
Taxable Income	18860
less Dividend	(1040)
	17820
1040 @ 10%	104
17820 @ 20% =	3564

Total Tax liability 3668

28040
25400   10500
  2640 ÷ 2 (1320)
          9180

Task 1.13

Shania has written to you with the following query:

'I am writing to you for some clarification on my father's tax affairs. He is no longer capable of handling his own money, and I have a letter of authorisation allowing me to deal with his tax matters.

I have received notification from HMRC of how much tax he has to pay for 31 January 2013. It says he owes £1,400 from 2011/12, and needs to pay £3,500 for 2012/13. I thought he had paid all the tax due for 2011/12, so I don't understand what the £1,400 is for. Also, I know that he has hardly any income this tax year, so where does the £3,500 come from?

If you could explain this to me, it would be much appreciated.'

You need to respond appropriately to her query.

Task 1.14

Using the following information, complete the tax return which follows (the 2011/12 version is shown):

Rachel sold 3 lots of listed shares during 2012/13. The summary information from these disposals is as follows:

Shares	Sale proceeds £	Cost £
August disposal	23,000	12,000
October disposal	14,000	10,000
February disposal	9,000	11,000

46,000   33,000

HM Revenue & Customs

Capital gains summary
Tax year 6 April 2011 to 5 April 2012

| 1 | Your name |
| | |

| 2 | Your Unique Taxpayer Reference (UTR) |

Summary of your enclosed computations

Read the notes on pages CGN 10 to CGN 12 before completing this section.

You must enclose your computations, including details of each gain or loss, as well as filling in the boxes.

3 Total gains *(Boxes 19+25+31+32)*

£ 15000 · 0 0

4 Gains qualifying for Entrepreneurs' Relief (but excluding gains deferred from before 23 June 2010) - *read the notes on page CGN 11*

£ · 0 0

5 Box 5 is not in use

6 Total losses of the year - *enter '0' if there are none*

£ 2000 · 0 0

7 Losses brought forward and used in the year

£ · 0 0

8 Adjustment to Capital Gains Tax - *see notes*

£ · 0 0

9 Additional liability in respect of non-resident or dual resident trusts

£ · 0 0

10 Losses available to be carried forward to later years

£ · 0 0

11 Losses used against an earlier year's gain (special circumstances apply - *read the notes on page CGN 12*)

£ · 0 0

12 Losses used against income - *amount claimed against 2011-12 income*

£ · 0 0

13 Losses used against income - *amount claimed against 2010-11 income*

£ · 0 0

14 Income losses of 2011-12 set against gains

£ · 0 0

15 Deferred gains from before 23 June 2010 qualifying for Entrepreneurs' Relief

£ · 0 0

Listed shares and securities

16 Number of disposals - *read the notes on page CGN 14*

3

17 Disposal proceeds

£ 46000 · 0 0

18 Allowable costs (including purchase price)

£ 33000 · 0 0

19 Gains in the year, before losses

£ 15000 · 0 0

20 If you are making any claim or election, put 'X' in the box

21 If your computations include any estimates or valuations, put 'X' in the box

Unlisted shares and securities

22 **Number of disposals** - *read the notes on page CGN 14*

23 **Disposal proceeds**

£ · 0 0

24 **Allowable costs (including purchase price)**

£ · 0 0

25 **Gains in the year, before losses**

£ · 0 0

26 **If you are making any claim or election, put 'X' in the box**

27 **If your computations include any estimates or valuations, put 'X' in the box**

Property and other assets and gains

28 **Number of disposals**

29 **Disposal proceeds**

£ · 0 0

30 **Allowable costs (including purchase price)**

£ · 0 0

31 **Gains in the year, before losses**

£ · 0 0

32 **Attributed gains where personal losses cannot be set off**

£ · 0 0

33 **Box 33 is not in use**

34 **If you are making any claim or election, put 'X' in the box**

35 **If your computations include any estimates or valuations, put 'X' in the box**

Any other information

36 **Please give any other information in this space**

Section 2

Task 2.1

Income from property is taxed on a receipts basis. | ~~True~~/False |

Task 2.2

Sue has two properties, details of which are as follows:

Three bedroom house:

(1) This unfurnished house is rented out for £800 per month. The property was occupied until 1 December when the tenants suddenly moved out, owing the rent for October and November. Sue knows she will not recover this rent. The property was let again from 1 March to another family. *a month*

(2) The only expense paid by Sue on the house was 6% commission to the agent on rent received.

Two bedroom flat:

(1) This furnished flat is rented out for £400 per month. The property was unoccupied until 1 June when a couple moved in on a twelve month lease.

(2) Sue paid council tax and water rates on the flat, totaling £1,400 for the tax year. She also paid insurance of £270.

Calculate the profit or loss made on each property, using the following table.

	Three bedroom house £	Two bedroom flat £
Income	5600	4000
Expenses:		
Commission	(336)	
Council Tax & Water		(1400)
Insurance		(270)
Wear & Tear		(260)
Total Profit	5264	2070

Task 2.3

(1)   The amount of rent you can receive which is tax free under the rent-a-room scheme is

£ 42 50

(options: £3,000; £3,500; £4,250; £4,500; £5,000)

(2)   Which of the following statements is true?

✓

	True	False
(a) You cannot use the rent-a-room scheme if you yourself live in rented accommodation.		✓
(b) A lodger can occupy an entire floor and the rent-a-room scheme still applies.	✓	
(c) The scheme applies to both furnished and unfurnished accommodation.		✓
(d) Charges for additional services, such as laundry, do not count in the annual exempt limit.		✓

(3)   Rent-a-room scheme cannot be claimed if the accommodation is also run as a guest house.

~~True~~/False

(4)   When working out the profit made from renting out a room, capital costs such as furniture cannot be taken into account

True/~~False~~

Task 2.4

For each statement, tick the appropriate box.

✓

	Actual Proceeds Used	Deemed proceeds used	No gain or loss basis
(1) Grandfather gives an asset to his granddaughter.		✓	
(2) Wife gives an asset to her husband.			✓
(3) Sarah sells an asset to her friend for £13,000 when the market value is £16,000.	✓		

Task 2.5

(1) Peter bought an asset in November 2005 for £180,000. He spent £40,000 on improving this asset in April 2007. He sold the asset for £250,000.

The gain on this asset is:

✓

(a) £250,000	
(b) £70,000	
(c) £120,000	
(d) £30,000	✓

(2) Andrea bought an asset in January 2000 for £26,000, selling it in December 2012 for £45,000. She paid auctioneers commission of 3% when she bought the asset and 5% when she sold the asset.

The gain on this asset is:

✓

(a) £20,470	
(b) £15,970	✓
(c) £17,530	
(d) £19,000	

Bought + commiss
|
26780 ⎤ - =15970
42750 ⎦
|
Sold - commiss.

(3) Advertising costs are not an allowable deduction as they are revenue expenses.

 True / ~~False~~

Task 2.6

Peter bought 10,000 shares in Lucky Ltd for £5 per share in October 2000. He received a bonus issue of 1 for 20 shares in March 2003. Recently, Peter sold 6,000 shares for £9 per share.

Clearly showing the balance of shares, and their value, to carry forward calculate the gain made on these shares. All workings must be shown in your calculations.

		£
October 2000	10,000 ×5	50,000
Bonus	10000÷20 = 500	0
	10 500	50000
Sold	(6000)	(28571)
Bal c/f	4500	21429
Proceeds.	6000 ×9	54000
Cost		(28571)
Gain		25429

50000×6000 ÷ 10500

Task 2.7

Match the statements listed below to the correct option in the table.

Asset	Sale proceeds	Cost	Statement
1	£4,000	£3,000	*Exempt Asset.*
2	£12,000	£8,000	*Calculate gain as normal.*
3	£7,000	£5,000	*Chattel marginal relief applies.*
4	£3,000	£8,000	*Sale proceeds deemed to be £6000*
5	£15,000	£21,000	*Calculate loss as normal*

Statements:

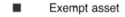

- Exempt asset
- Calculate gain as normal
- Calculate loss as normal
- Sale proceeds deemed to be £6,000
- Chattel marginal relief applies

Task 2.8

Rebecca bought a house on 1 January 1997 for £70,000. She lived in the house until 31 December 2001 when she moved in with her elderly parents. The house remained unoccupied until she sold it on 1 June 2012 for £205,000. This house is Rebecca's only property.

Which periods are treated as occupied and which are not?

Occupation / Deemed Occupation	Non-occupation
1/1/1997 – 31/12/2001 1/6/2009 – 1/6/2012	1/1/2002 – 31/5/2009

Task 2.9

(1)   The annual exemption is applied before capital losses are deducted.

   ~~True~~ /False

(2)   Excess capital losses cannot be set against other taxable income.

   True / ~~False~~

(3)   Capital gains are taxed at 28% for higher rate tax payers.

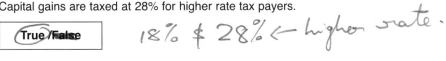   True / ~~False~~   18% & 28% ← higher rate.

Personal taxation

Practice assessment 3

Section 1

Task 1.1

State whether each of the following statements is true or false.   ✓

		True	False
(a)	An individual can correct information submitted on a tax return up to a maximum of four years after the end of the tax year.	✓	
(b)	All taxpayers must submit their income tax returns online.		✓

Task 1.2

State whether each of the following statements is true or false.

✓

		True	False
(a)	Taxpayers must inform HMRC about new sources of taxable income by 5th October following the end of the tax year.	✓	
(b)	The penalty for failing to keep appropriate records is up £3,000 for each tax year.	✓	
(c)	There is no penalty for making an error in a tax return provided the taxpayer took reasonable care.	✓	
(d)	When an accountant is advising a client the greatest duty of care is to HMRC.		✓
(e)	HMRC only has powers to visit the premises of taxpayers, not their agents.		✓
(f)	If a taxpayer finds that he has made an error (that he has no reason to believe HMRC has discovered) in a tax return and informs HMRC, this is considered to be an unprompted disclosure.	✓	

Task 1.3

Select from the following list, those that indicate a contract for services.

			✓
(a)	Choose work hours and invoice for work done		✓
(b)	Usually work for one employer		
(c)	Told how, where and when to do work		
(d)	No risk of capital		
(e)	Decide yourself how, when and where to do work		✓
(f)	Can employ helper or substitute		✓
(g)	Equipment is provided		
(h)	Bear losses from work that is not to standard		✓
(i)	Work set hours and paid regular wage with sick pay and holidays		
(j)	Provide own equipment		✓

Task 1.4

Jane has provided you with the following information regarding her employment. _7 months_

She is paid monthly. Her annual salary was £24,600 for the year ended 31 October 2012, and £25,800 for the year ended 31 October 2013. _5 months_

She received a bonus of £1,100 on 15 December 2012. This related to the year ended 31 October 2012. She received a bonus of £750 on 20 December 2013. This related to the year ended 31 October 2013.

The company paid a pension contribution of 6% of her total employment pay into the company pension scheme.

Complete the following with respect to the tax year 2012/13.

The taxable salary (excluding bonus) is £ 25100   14350
                                                  + 10 750

The taxable bonus is £ 1100

The company contribution to the pension scheme is £ 1572

The total assessable employment income for Jane is £ 26200

Task 1.5

Dirk is a senior manager in the defence industry. During the tax year he was provided with the following company cars:　*3 months*

From the start of the tax year until 30 June he was provided with a Jaguar. It was purchased for £41,000 second hand, and had a list price of £52,000. Its emissions were 152 g/km and it was powered by a petrol engine.

Following a promotion for Dirk, the Jaguar was replaced with a new diesel powered Range Rover on 1 July. This car had a list price of £72,000. The company believed that Dirk's new role placed him at increased risk of a terrorism attack, and paid £25,000 for the Range Rover to be equipped with bullet resistant glass and strengthened bodywork. The emissions of the car were 230 g/km. On 1 December the car was fitted with passengers' televisions so that Dirk's family could be entertained on long trips. This cost the company £1,200.

Complete the following table to show the 2012/13 benefit in kind arising from the use of these cars. Ignore any benefit arising from private fuel.

Car	Percentage applicable based on CO_2 emissions %	Cost of car used in benefit calculation £	Benefit in kind £
Jaguar	21%	52000	2730
Range Rover	35%	73200	19215
Total			21945

Task 1.6

(a) Place a tick in the appropriate column of the table below to show whether each of the items listed would or would not result in an assessable benefit in kind for an employee.

✓

The following are provided by the employer to the employee	Benefit in kind	No benefit in kind
Use of a company credit card to pay for the entertainment of customers (with approval of the employer)		✓
Mileage payment for use of employee's own motorcycle for business purposes at a rate of 24p per mile		✓
Petrol for travel from home to work in a company car	✓	
Training costs including course and examination fees for accountancy trainee undertaking AAT course		✓

(b) Calculate the assessable benefit in kind (in whole pounds) for each of the following:

	Benefit £
On 6 April an employee was provided with an interest free loan of £15,000. During the tax year he made three repayments, each of £2,000. The remainder of the loan was still outstanding at the end of the tax year.	480
On 6 April an employee was allowed the use of a home cinema system that had previously been used by the company. The home cinema had originally cost the company £1,500, but its market value on 1 December was £1,000.	200

15000
3×2000 = 9000
      24000
24000 ÷2 = 12000
12000 × 4% = 480
1000 × 20% = 200

Task 1.7

Using the following table, analyse the benefits into those that are exempt from tax, and those that are taxable.

✓

Description	Exempt	Taxable
Provision of a chauffeur for business and private journeys		✓
Long service award in cash for employee with 10 year's service		✓
Counselling services	✓	
Free meals in a staff restaurant available to all staff	✓	
Provision of free UK health insurance		✓

Task 1.8

Tick the appropriate box to show whether each of the following situations would increase or reduce an employee's tax liability under the approved mileage allowance payments scheme.

✓

Business mileage and rate paid	Increase tax liability	Reduce tax liability
5,000 miles at 50p per mile	✓	
15,000 miles at 45p per mile	✓	
15,000 miles at 38p per mile		✓
20,000 miles at 25p per mile		✓

Empl 5000 × 0.50 = 2500 ↑
HMRC 5000 × 0.45 = 2250

HMRC 10000 × 0.45 = 4500
5000 × 0.25 = 1250
5750

Emp 15000 × 0.45 = 6750

Emp 15000 × 0.38 = 5700
HMRC 10000 × 0.45 = 4500
5000 × 0.25 = 1250
5750

Empl 20000 × 0.25 = 5000
HMRC 10000 × 0.45 = 4500
10000 × 0.25 = 2500
7000

Task 1.9

Kerry has received the amounts shown on the following table from various investments. Complete the table to show the assessable amounts and the amounts of tax that are treated as having been paid.

Investment	Amount Received £	Assessable Amount £	Tax treated as paid £
Bank deposit account	1,600	·2000	400
Premium bonds	2,000	—	—
Cash ISA	270	—	—
NS&I guaranteed growth bond	800	1000	200
Government stocks (gilts)	1,200	1200	—
Totals	5,870	4200	600

Task 1.10

Jo is a taxpayer whose amount of general income means that she pays tax at the additional rate. She received £3,600 in UK dividends.

Complete the following table in respect of the dividend income:

	Assessable amount £	Total tax liability £
Dividends received of £3,600	4000	1700

Task 1.11

Using the following table, analyse the income into whether it is exempt from tax, or taxable.

Description	Exempt	Taxable
Gratuities (tips) received in cash		✓
Winnings from local lottery	✓	

Task 1.12

During the tax year, Jennifer had employment income of £127,500 and received dividends of £900 (net).

She paid £16,000 (net) into a personal pension scheme.

Calculate her total income tax liability (i.e. before deduction of tax paid), using the blank table given below.

Employment Income		127500
Dividend		1000
	Total Income	128500
Personal Allowance		(3855)
Taxable Income		124645
Tax on General Income		
(34370 + 20000)	54370 @ 20%	10874
(127500 - 3855 - 54370)	69275 @ 40%	27710
Tax On Dividends	1000 @ 32·5%	325
Tax Liability		38,909

Handwritten side notes:

28500
(20,000) PP
108500
100,000)
8500 × 50%
= 4250
105 - 4250 =
855

Task 1.13

The company that you work for has recently arranged for payroll giving to be available for all staff so that they can donate to charities.

Write an email to all staff that explains how payroll giving works and compares it with the gift aid scheme.

email
from:
to:
subject:
date:

Task 1.14

Jack Price is employed by PPP Limited. His P60 for the tax year showed pay of £44,600 and tax deducted of £9,100.

He was provided with a company car with an assessable benefit amount of £3,000 and fuel for private motoring with an assessable amount of £3,030.

He paid out and reclaimed from his employer business travel expenses of £380 during the tax year. The employer does not hold an HMRC dispensation for such payments.

Complete the relevant sections of the Employment tax return page for Jack. The form is reproduced on the next page.

HM Revenue & Customs

Employment

Tax year 6 April 2011 to 5 April 2012

Your name

Your Unique Taxpayer Reference (UTR)

Complete an *Employment* page for each employment or directorship

1 Pay from this employment – the total from your P45 or P60 – *before tax was taken off*

£ [   ] · 0 0

2 UK tax taken off pay in box 1

£ [   ] · 0 0

3 Tips and other payments not on your P60 – *read page EN 4 of the notes*

£ [   ] · 0 0

4 PAYE tax reference of your employer (on your P45/P60)

[   ] / [   ]

5 Your employer's name

6 If you were a company director, put 'X' in the box

7 And, if the company was a close company, put 'X' in the box

8 If you are a part-time teacher in England or Wales and are on the Repayment of Teachers' Loans Scheme for this employment, put 'X' in the box

Benefits from your employment – use your form P11D (or equivalent information)

9 Company cars and vans – *the total 'cash equivalent' amount*

£ [   ] · 0 0

10 Fuel for company cars and vans – *the total 'cash equivalent' amount*

£ [   ] · 0 0

11 Private medical and dental insurance – *the total 'cash equivalent' amount*

£ [   ] · 0 0

12 Vouchers, credit cards and excess mileage allowance

£ [   ] · 0 0

13 Goods and other assets provided by your employer – *the total value or amount*

£ [   ] · 0 0

14 Accommodation provided by your employer – *the total value or amount*

£ [   ] · 0 0

15 Other benefits (including interest-free and low interest loans) – *the total 'cash equivalent' amount*

£ [   ] · 0 0

16 Expenses payments received and balancing charges

£ [   ] · 0 0

Employment expenses

17 Business travel and subsistence expenses

£ [   ] · 0 0

18 Fixed deductions for expenses

£ [   ] · 0 0

19 Professional fees and subscriptions

£ [   ] · 0 0

20 Other expenses and capital allowances

£ [   ] · 0 0

ⓘ **Shares schemes, employment lump sums, compensation, deductions and Seafarers' Earnings Deduction** are on the *Additional information* pages enclosed in the tax return pack

Section 2

Task 2.1

Select whether the following statement is true or false:

If a taxpayer has property income related to both furnished holiday lettings and other lettings, the income from each of these two categories must be disclosed separately to HMRC.

 TRUE / FALSE

Task 2.2

Analyse the following expenses into whether they are an allowable deduction in calculating UK property income or not by ticking the appropriate column.

✓

	Allowable deduction	Not an allowable deduction
Depreciation of property		✓
Monthly repayment of mortgage capital		✓
Advertising for tenants	✓	
Repainting windows	✓	
Insurance against irrecoverable rent	✓	
Installing central heating		✓
Capital allowances related to holiday lettings	✓	

Task 2.3

(a) Indicate with a tick whether each of the following statements related to property income is true or false. ✓

	True	False
If a taxpayer is claiming rent a room relief he cannot claim any other deductions from the rental income	✓	
The time limit to claim rent a room relief is one year after the due date for the online tax return	✓	

(b) Jessica has a furnished cottage that she rents out to holiday makers. During the tax year it was available for letting from 1 May until 31 October. It was unoccupied for two weeks during this period.

Does this qualify as a furnished holiday letting? Tick one statement.

✓

Statement	
Yes, this qualifies	
No, this doesn't qualify only because it was not actually let for long enough	
No, this doesn't qualify only because it wasn't available for letting for long enough	✓
No, this doesn't qualify because it was neither available nor actually let for long enough	

Task 2.4

For each statement in connection with capital gains, tick the appropriate box.

✓

	True	False
Payment of capital gains tax is subject to the same rules regarding payments on account as income tax		✓
The annual exempt amount for capital gains tax is increased for taxpayers over the age of 65		✓

Task 2.5

14840

A taxpayer had previously bought an asset for £14,000, plus 6% auction commission. He sold it during the tax year for £15,000, having spent £100 to advertise it for sale. The cost of insuring the asset during his ownership was £150.

Calculate the gain or loss using the following computation.

	Amount £
Proceeds	15000
Total costs	14940
Gain / Loss	60.

Task 2.6

Paul bought 18,000 shares in Leicester Ltd for £4.50 per share in October 2000. In April 2012 he took up a rights issue of 4 for 9 at £3 per share. In January 2013, Paul sold 12,000 shares for £6 per share.

Clearly showing the balance of shares, and their value, to carry forward calculate the gain made on these shares. All workings must be shown in your calculations.

		£
Oct 2000	18000	81000
April 2012	8000	24000
Total	26000	105000
Jan 2013 Sold.	(12000)	(48462)
	14,000	56538
Proceeds.		72000
Cost		(48462)
Gain		23538.

Task 2.7

Complete the following table to show which statements are true and which are false in connection with capital gains tax.

✓

Statement	True	False
Gifts to charities are exempt from capital gains tax	✓	
Gifts between a father and son are exempt from capital gains tax		✓
When applying the 5/3 restriction to chattels, the proceeds figure used is before any costs of sale are deducted	✓	
Chattels are defined as tangible moveable property	✓	
Non-wasting chattels are exempt from capital gains tax		✓

Task 2.8

Emily bought a house on 1 January 2000. She lived in the house until 31 December 2003 when she moved abroad to Dubai to take up a job. She worked there until 30 September 2007, while renting out her own house. She then moved back into her own house from 1 October 2007 until 31 December 2009, when she moved to a new home and put the house on the market. The house was eventually sold on 31 March 2013.

Which periods are treated as occupied and which are not?

Occupation / Deemed Occupation	Non-occupation
1/1/2000 – 31/12/2003 1/1/2004 – 30/9/2007 1/10/2007 – 31/12/2009 1/4/2010 – 31/3/2013	1/1/2010 – 31/3/2010

Task 2.9

Complete the following sentences.

A taxpayer had capital losses brought forward of £6,000. During the tax year he made two disposals, making a gain of £16,300 on one and a loss of £1,900 on the other.

The amount subject to capital gains tax for the year (after the annual exempt amount) will be

0

16 300
(10 600)
5700

The capital loss to be carried forward to be set against future gains will be

2200

6000
+1900
7900
- 5700

Practice assessment 1 – answers

Section 1

Task 1.1

(b)   is true

Task 1.2

(c) and (e) are true

Task 1.3

The following indicate employment.

(a)	The contract is a contract of service	✓
(b)	Choose work hours and invoice for work done	
(c)	Told how, where and when to do work	✓
(d)	No risk of capital	✓
(e)	Decide yourself how, when and where to do work	
(f)	Can employ helper or substitute	
(g)	Equipment is provided	✓
(h)	Bear losses from work that is not to standard	
(i)	Work set hours and paid regular wage with sick pay and holidays	✓
(j)	Usually work for one employer	✓
(k)	Provide own equipment	

Task 1.4

The taxable salary (excluding bonus) is £22,300

The taxable bonus is £1,200

The company contribution to the pension scheme is £1,410

The total assessable employment income for Jenny is £23,500

Task 1.5

(1)   (a)   99 g/km   10%
          (b)   140 g/km   19%
          (c)   171 g/km   25%
          (d)   241 g/km   35%

(2)   (a)   The cost of the car used in the benefit in kind computation is £16,000

          (b)   The percentage used in the benefit in kind computation is 24%

          (c)   The assessable benefit for Steve relating to the car for 2012/13 is £1,600

Task 1.6

   (1)   (b)   £75,000

   (2)

		Yes	No
(a)	House provided for a finance director		✓
(b)	House provided by employer for librarian working for local authority		✓
(c)	Flat in nursing home provided for an on-site nursing manager	✓	

   (3)   (c)   £8,700   *(£6,300 + (4% x £50,000) + (20% x £2,000))*

Task 1.7

Description	Exempt	Taxable
Interest-free loans not exceeding £5,000	✓	
Cash payment to employee to help with childcare costs		✓
Employer contributions to company pension scheme	✓	
Free meals in a staff restaurant only available to senior managers		✓
Performance related bonus payment		✓
Provision of one mobile telephone and its running costs	✓	
Holiday pay		✓
Use of a bicycle and helmet to commute to work	✓	
Childcare vouchers up to £55 per week for basic rate taxpayers	✓	

Task 1.8

   (1)   (a)   She will have a taxable amount of £500.

   (2)   (b)   Her taxable salary will be reduced by £2,364.

   (3)   (c)   A taxable amount of £80.

   (4)   (d)   Geraldine's basic rate band is extended by £3,000.

Task 1.9

Investment	Amount Received £	Assessable Amount £	Tax treated as paid £
Building Society Account	1,500	1,875	375
Dividends from UK Cos.	4,950	5,500	550
Stocks & Shares ISA	190	0	0
NS&I investment account	400	400	0
Local authority loan interest	1,600	2,000	400
Totals	8,640	9,775	1,325

Task 1.10

(a) Government Stocks (Gilts)	
(b) NS&I Easy Access Account	
(c) NS&I Index-linked Savings Certificates	✓
(d) NS&I Fixed Interest Savings Certificates	✓
(e) Cash ISA	✓
(f) Unquoted company loans	

Task 1.11

Total ISA limit	(e) £11,280
Cash ISA limit	(b) £5,640

Task 1.12

	£
Pension Income	102,000
Bank Interest	750
Sub Total	102,750
Personal Allowance	7,230
Taxable Income	95,520
Tax:	
General (£34,370 + £1,000) x 20%	7,074
(£94,770 − £35,370) x 40%	23,760
Savings £750 x 40%	300
Tax Liability	31,134

Although James is 77 years old his income is too high for him to benefit from the aged allowance. As his adjusted net income is over £100,000 the basic allowance is restricted.

Personal Allowance Working:

Basic Allowance	£8,105
Less ((£102,750 - £1,000) - £100,000) x 50%	£875
	£7,230

Task 1.13

email	
To	All Staff
From	Accounting Technician
Subject	Comparison of Tax Implications of Travelling Schemes
date:	XX

You are aware that there is to be a new scheme for business journeys. I want to explain how the tax implications for you compare with the previous scheme.

Under the old scheme you were paid 50p per mile for all business journeys that you undertook in your own car. HMRC rates were lower than this, at 45p per mile for the first 10,000 miles in a tax year, and 25p per mile for any additional miles. This means that up until now you will have paid tax on the difference between the amount that you received and the HMRC rates.

The good news is that under the new pool car scheme there is no tax liability for using the car for business journeys. As you know, the company will also reimburse you for the cost of petrol that you fill up a pool car with, and there will be no tax implications for this either.

Task 1.14

(a)

	£	£
Income		10,000
Expenditure:		
Council Tax	720	
Water Rates	260	
Insurance	280	
Managing Agent's Charges	800	
Wear & Tear Allowance	902	
		2,962
Assessable Income		7,038

(b) *reproduced opposite*

Section 2

Task 2.1   (a) and (c) are true

Task 2.2

	Two bedroom house £	One bedroom flat £
Income	9,400	5,880
Expenses:		
Redecoration	1,510	
Management Charge	1,128	
Council Tax & Rates		1,160
Insurance		370
Wear & tear Allowance		472
Assessable Profit	6,762	3,878

Property income

Do not include furnished holiday lettings, Real Estate Investment Trust or Property Authorised Investment Funds dividends/distributions here.

20 Total rents and other income from property

£ 1 0 0 0 0 . 0 0

21 Tax taken off any income in box 20

£ . 0 0

22 Premiums for the grant of a lease - *from box E on the Working Sheet on page UKPN 8 of the notes.*

£ . 0 0

23 Reverse premiums and inducements

£ . 0 0

Property expenses

24 Rent, rates, insurance, ground rents etc.

£ 1 2 6 0 . 0 0

25 Property repairs, maintenance and renewals

£ . 0 0

26 Loan interest and other financial costs

£ . 0 0

27 Legal, management and other professional fees

£ 8 0 0 . 0 0

28 Costs of services provided, including wages

£ . 0 0

29 Other allowable property expenses

£ . 0 0

Calculating your taxable profit or loss

30 Private use adjustment - *read page UKPN 9 of the notes*

£ . 0 0

31 Balancing charges - *read page UKPN 10 of the notes*

£ . 0 0

32 Annual Investment Allowance

£ . 0 0

33 Business Premises Renovation Allowance (Assisted Areas only) - *read page UKPN 11 of the notes*

£ . 0 0

34 All other capital allowances

£ . 0 0

35 Landlord's Energy Saving Allowance

£ . 0 0

36 10% wear and tear allowance - *for furnished residential accommodation only*

£ 9 0 2 . 0 0

37 Rent a Room exempt amount

£ . 0 0

38 Adjusted profit for the year - *from box O on the Working Sheet on page UKPN 16*

£ 7 0 3 8 . 0 0

39 Loss brought forward used against this year's profits

£ . 0 0

40 Taxable profit for the year (box 38 minus box 39)

£ 7 0 3 8 . 0 0

41 Adjusted loss for the year - *from box O on the Working Sheet on page UKPN 16*

£ . 0 0

42 Loss set off against 2011-12 total income - *this will be unusual - read page UKPN 15 of the notes*

£ . 0 0

43 Loss to carry forward to following year, including unused losses brought forward

£ . 0 0

Task 2.3

(1)

	Claiming rent a room relief £	Normal rental income computation £
Income	13,520	13,520
Allowable deductions:		
Rent a room relief	4,250	
Heating		170
Food		1,456
Wear & tear allowance		1,352
Assessable amount	9,270	10,542

(2) To pay the minimum income tax, Mike should **claim** rent a room relief.

Task 2.4

	Actual Proceeds Used	Deemed proceeds used	No gain or loss basis
(1) Dave gives an asset to his father		✓	
(2) Peter sells an asset to his friend	✓		
(3) Simon gives an asset to his friend		✓	

Task 2.5

(a) The gain on the asset is £11,500

(b) The amount of loss that will be relieved is £900

(c) The capital gains tax payable is £0

(d) The loss to be carried forward to the next tax year is £1,600

Task 2.6

	Number of Shares	Value £
Purchase	25,000	125,000
Rights	15,000	60,000
Sub total	40,000	185,000
Disposal	10,000	46,250
Balance	30,000	138,750
Proceeds		80,000
Cost		46,250
Gain		33,750

Task 2.7

Asset	Exempt	Chargeable
Land		✓
Principal private residence	✓	
Antique painting		✓
Unquoted shares		✓
Caravan	✓	
Government securities	✓	
Classic car	✓	
Horse	✓	

Task 2.8

Occupation / Deemed Occupation	Non-occupation
1/1/1999 – 31/12/2002	
1/1/2003 – 30/6/2006	
1/7/2006 – 31/12/2010	
1/1/2011– 1/3/2013	

Task 2.9

All the statements are false.

Practice assessment 2 – answers

Section 1

Task 1.1

Both the statements are **false.**

Task 1.2

   (1)   (d)

   (2)   (c)

Task 1.3

	Employment	Self Employment
Contract of service is for:	✓	
Contract for service is for:		✓
A high level of control by an employer over the work performed would indicate what type of relationship?	✓	

Task 1.4

   (a)   £18,930

   (b)   £876

   (c)   £946.50

Task 1.5

   (1)   **(a)**   13%

           (b)   17%

           (c)   20%

           (d)   35%

   (2)   **(a)**   £21,000

           (b)   30%

           (c)   £6,300

Task 1.6

    (1)   (b)

    (2)   (c)

    (3)

		Yes	No
(a)	Accommodation provided for a caretaker of a school	✓	
(b)	Accommodation provided for security reasons	✓	
(c)	Accommodation provided for all directors		✓

    (4)   (a)   £3,000

    (5)   (a) and (d) are correct.

Task 1.7

    (1)   £55

    (2)   1

    (3)   £50

    (4)   £8,000

Task 1.8

    (1)   (d)

    (2)   (a)

    (3)   (c)

    (4)   (a)

Task 1.9

    (1)

Received net	Received gross
Interest from bank accounts	Interest from NS&I investment accounts
Interest from building society accounts	Gilts
Loan stock from unquoted companies	NS&I income bonds

    (2)   (a)   £80

Task 1.10

    (a)   £24

    (b)   £240

Task 1.11

    (a)   £11,280

    (b)   True

Task 1.12

	£
Income	27,000
Gross dividends	1,040
	28,040
Personal allowance	9,180
Taxable income	18,860
Tax:	
£17,820 x 20%	3,564
£1040 x 10%	104
	3,668
Personal Allowance:	
Age allowance	£10,500
less (£28,040 – £25,400) x 50%	£1,320
	£9,180

Task 1.13

Half of the tax liability for any year is paid by 31 January in that tax year, and the other half is paid by 31 July following the tax year. This is based on an estimate, using the preceding tax years' liability. Therefore, when your father paid his tax liability on 31 January 2012 and 31 July 2012 for 2011/12, this was based on his liability for the previous year.

When the final figures were sent to HMRC, they worked out that these two instalments were not enough to cover the full liability; hence the £1,400 is the balance of tax due.

As explained, the instalment on 31 January 2013 for this current tax year is based on the actual liability for the previous year, 2011/12. If the instalments he pays for 2012/13 exceed his actual liability, ie he overpays for 2012/13, he will receive a refund from HMRC.

However, he can claim to reduce these instalments if he knows that his income will not be as high as it was last year. Whilst this is fine, your father needs to be careful. If he makes an incorrect claim to reduce these instalments, HMRC will charge him interest on the difference between what should have been paid and what he actually paid.

Task 1.14

See completed form opposite. (*Note that page two is blank for the purposes of this task.*)

HM Revenue & Customs

Capital gains summary
Tax year 6 April 2011 to 5 April 2012

1 Your name

RACHEL

2 Your Unique Taxpayer Reference (UTR)

Summary of your enclosed computations

Read the notes on pages CGN 10 to CGN 12 before completing this section.

You must enclose your computations, including details of each gain or loss, as well as filling in the boxes.

3 Total gains *(Boxes 19+25+31+32)*

£ 1 5 0 0 0 · 0 0

4 Gains qualifying for Entrepreneurs' Relief (but excluding gains deferred from before 23 June 2010) - *read the notes on page CGN 11*

£ · 0 0

5 Box 5 is not in use

6 Total losses of the year - *enter '0' if there are none*

£ 2 0 0 0 · 0 0

7 Losses brought forward and used in the year

£ · 0 0

8 Adjustment to Capital Gains Tax - *see notes*

£ — · 0 0

9 Additional liability in respect of non-resident or dual resident trusts

£ · 0 0

10 Losses available to be carried forward to later years

£ · 0 0

11 Losses used against an earlier year's gain (special circumstances apply - *read the notes on page CGN 12*)

£ · 0 0

12 Losses used against income - *amount claimed against 2011-12 income*

£ · 0 0

13 Losses used against income - *amount claimed against 2010-11 income*

£ · 0 0

14 Income losses of 2011-12 set against gains

£ · 0 0

15 Deferred gains from before 23 June 2010 qualifying for Entrepreneurs' Relief

£ · 0 0

Listed shares and securities

16 Number of disposals - *read the notes on page CGN 14*

3

17 Disposal proceeds

£ 4 6 0 0 0 · 0 0

18 Allowable costs (including purchase price)

£ 3 3 0 0 0 · 0 0

19 Gains in the year, before losses

£ 1 5 0 0 0 · 0 0

20 If you are making any claim or election, put 'X' in the box

21 If your computations include any estimates or valuations, put 'X' in the box

Section 2

Task 2.1

False.

Task 2.2

	Three bedroom house £	Two bedroom flat £
Income*	5,600	4,000
Expenses:		
Commission	336	
Council tax and rates		1,400
Insurance		270
Wear & tear allowance		260
Profits	5,264	2,070

* The gross income for the house could alternatively be shown here, with the irrecoverable rent shown as an expense.

Task 2.3

(1) £4,250

(2) (b) is true

(3) False

(4) True

Task 2.4

	Actual Proceeds Used	Deemed proceeds used	No gain or loss basis
(1) Grandfather gives an asset to his granddaughter.		✓	
(2) Wife gives an asset to her husband.			✓
(3) Sarah sells an asset to her friend for £13,000 when the market value is £16,000.	✓		

Task 2.5

    (1)   (d)   £30,000

    (2)   (b)   £15,970

    (3)   False.

Task 2.6

	Number of shares	£
October 2000	10,000	50,000
Bonus	500	
Sub total	10,500	50,000
Disposal	6,000	28,571
Pool Balance	4,500	21,429
Proceeds		54,000
Cost		28,571
Gain		25,429

Task 2.7

Asset	Sale proceeds	Cost	Statement
1	£4,000	£3,000	Exempt asset
2	£12,000	£8,000	Calculate gain as normal
3	£7,000	£5,000	Chattel marginal relief applies
4	£3,000	£8,000	Sale proceeds deemed to be £6,000
5	£15,000	£21,000	Calculate loss as normal

Task 2.8

Occupation / Deemed Occupation	Non-occupation
1/1/1997 - 31/12/2001 1/6/2009 - 1/6/2012	1/1/2002 - 31/5/2009

Task 2.9

    (1)   False

    (2)   True

    (3)   True

Practice assessment 3 – answers

Section 1

Task 1.1

  (a)   True

  (b)   False

Task 1.2

  (a)   True

  (b)   True

  (c)   True

  (d)   False

  (e)   False

  (f)   True

Task 1.3

Contracts for services are indicated by:

  (a)   Choose work hours and invoice for work done

  (e)   Decide yourself how, when and where to do work

  (f)   Can employ helper or substitute

  (h)   Bear losses from work that is not to standard

  (j)   Provide own equipment

Task 1.4

The taxable salary (excluding bonus) is £25,100

The taxable bonus is £1,100

The company contribution to the pension scheme is £1,572

The total assessable employment income for Jane is £26,200

Task 1.5

Car	Percentage applicable based on CO_2 emissions %	Cost of car used in benefit calculation £	Benefit in kind £
Jaguar	21	52,000	2,730
Range Rover	35	73,200	19,215
Total			21,945

Task 1.6

(a)

The following are provided by the employer to the employee	Benefit in kind	No benefit in kind
Use of a company credit card to pay for the entertainment of customers (with approval of the employer)		✓
Mileage payment for use of employee's own motorcycle for business purposes at a rate of 24p per mile		✓
Petrol for travel from home to work in a company car	✓	
Training costs including course and examination fees for accountancy trainee undertaking AAT course		✓

(b)

	Benefit £
On 6 April an employee was provided with an interest free loan of £15,000. During the tax year he made three repayments, each of £2,000. The remainder of the loan was still outstanding at the end of the tax year.	480
On 6 April an employee was allowed the use of a home cinema system that had previously been used by the company. The home cinema had originally cost the company £1,500, but its market value on 1 December was £1,000.	200

Task 1.7

Description	Exempt	Taxable
Provision of a chauffeur for business and private journeys		✓
Long service award in cash for employee with 10 year's service		✓
Counselling services	✓	
Free meals in a staff restaurant available to all staff	✓	
Provision of free UK health insurance		✓

Task 1.8

Business mileage and rate paid	Increase tax liability	Reduce tax liability
5,000 miles at 50p per mile	✓	
15,000 miles at 45p per mile	✓	
15,000 miles at 38p per mile		✓
20,000 miles at 25p per mile		✓

Task 1.9

Investment	Amount Received	Assessable Amount	Tax treated as paid
	£	£	£
Bank deposit account	1,600	2,000	400
Premium bonds	2,000	0	0
Cash ISA	270	0	0
NS&I guaranteed growth bond	800	1,000	200
Government stocks (gilts)	1,200	1,200	0
Totals	5,870	4,200	600

Task 1.10

	Assessable amount	Total tax liability
	£	£
Dividends received of £3,600	4,000	1,700

Task 1.11

Description	Exempt	Taxable
Gratuities (tips) received in cash		✓
Winnings from local lottery	✓	

Task 1.12

		£
Employment Income		127,500
Dividends		1,000
		128,500
Personal Allowance	(See below)	3,855
Taxable		124,645
Tax on general income:		
(£34,370 + £20,000)	£54,370 at 20%	10,874
(£127,500 -£3,855 - £54,370)	£69,275 at 40%	27,710
Tax on dividends	£1,000 at 32.5%	325
Tax liability		38,909
Workings:	Basic Personal Allowance	8,105
Less	50% (£128,500 - £20,000 - £100,000)	4,250
		3,855

Task 1.13

---

email

from: Accounting Technician

to: All staff

subject: Payroll Giving Scheme

date: XX/XX/XXXX

I am writing to explain the payroll giving scheme that the company is now operating.

The scheme is entirely voluntary, but any member of staff may use it to make regular donations to a charity of their choice. The payroll department will arrange to deduct a regular amount that you choose from your income before income tax is calculated on the balance. This will give you full tax relief from any donations, so for example a payment of £50 per month would only actually cost you £40 per month if you are a basic rate (20%) taxpayer. If you were paying tax at higher than the basic rate the cost to you of the same donation would be even less.

This scheme provides the same level of tax relief as the gift aid scheme that you may have heard of. Gift aid does not operate through the payroll, but allows individuals to make one-off or regular donations to charity net of a 20% tax deduction. This means that a donation by a basic rate taxpayer of £50 would again only cost £40. Higher rate taxpayers would receive additional tax relief through an increase in the basic rate band by the gross amount of the donation, so less tax is paid at the higher rate.

You can use either or both schemes if you wish to donate to charity.

Task 1.14

HM Revenue & Customs

Employment
Tax year 6 April 2011 to 5 April 2012

Your name

JACK PRICE

Your Unique Taxpayer Reference (UTR)

Complete an *Employment* page for each employment or directorship

1 Pay from this employment – the total from your P45 or P60 - *before tax was taken off*

£ 4 4 6 0 0 · 0 0

2 UK tax taken off pay in box 1

£ 9 1 0 0 · 0 0

3 Tips and other payments not on your P60
- *read page EN 4 of the notes*

£ · 0 0

4 PAYE tax reference of your employer (on your P45/P60)

/

5 Your employer's name

PPP LIMITED

6 If you were a company director, put 'X' in the box

7 And, if the company was a close company, put 'X' in the box

8 If you are a part-time teacher in England or Wales and are on the Repayment of Teachers' Loans Scheme for this employment, put 'X' in the box

Benefits from your employment - use your form P11D (or equivalent information)

9 Company cars and vans - *the total 'cash equivalent' amount*

£ 3 0 0 0 · 0 0

10 Fuel for company cars and vans
- *the total 'cash equivalent' amount*

£ 3 0 3 0 · 0 0

11 Private medical and dental insurance
- *the total 'cash equivalent' amount*

£ · 0 0

12 Vouchers, credit cards and excess mileage allowance

£ · 0 0

13 Goods and other assets provided by your employer
- *the total value or amount*

£ · 0 0

14 Accommodation provided by your employer
- *the total value or amount*

£ · 0 0

15 Other benefits (including interest-free and low interest loans) - *the total 'cash equivalent' amount*

£ · 0 0

16 Expenses payments received and balancing charges

£ 3 8 0 · 0 0

Employment expenses

17 Business travel and subsistence expenses

£ 3 8 0 · 0 0

18 Fixed deductions for expenses

£ · 0 0

19 Professional fees and subscriptions

£ · 0 0

20 Other expenses and capital allowances

£ · 0 0

ⓘ Shares schemes, employment lump sums, compensation, deductions and Seafarers' Earnings Deduction are on the
Additional information pages enclosed in the tax return pack.

Section 2

Task 2.1

TRUE

Task 2.2

	Allowable deduction	**Not an allowable deduction**
Depreciation of property		✓
Monthly repayment of mortgage capital		✓
Advertising for tenants	✓	
Repainting windows	✓	
Insurance against irrecoverable rent	✓	
Installing central heating		✓
Capital allowances related to holiday lettings	✓	

Task 2.3

(a)

	True	*False*
If a taxpayer is claiming rent a room relief he cannot claim any other deductions from the rental income	✓	
The time limit to claim rent a room relief is one year after the due date for the online tax return	✓	

(b)

Statement	
Yes, this qualifies	
No, this doesn't qualify only because it was not actually let for long enough	
No, this doesn't qualify only because it wasn't available for letting for long enough	✓
No, this doesn't qualify because it was neither available nor actually let for long enough	

Task 2.4

	True	False
Payment of capital gains tax is subject to the same rules regarding payments on account as income tax		✓
The annual exempt amount for capital gains tax is increased for taxpayers over the age of 65		✓

Task 2.5

	Amount £
Proceeds	15,000
Total costs	14,940
Gain	60

Task 2.6

October 2000	18,000	£81,000
April 2012	8,000	£24,000
	26,000	£105,000
Disposal	12,000	£48,462
Pool balance	14,000	£56,538
Proceeds		£72,000
Cost		£48,462
Gain		£23,538

Task 2.7

Statement	True	False
Gifts to charities are exempt from capital gains tax	✓	
Gifts between a father and son are exempt from capital gains tax		✓
When applying the 5/3 restriction to chattels, the proceeds figure used is before any costs of sale are deducted	✓	
Chattels are defined as tangible moveable property	✓	
Non-wasting chattels are exempt from capital gains tax		✓

Task 2.8

Occupation / Deemed Occupation	Non-occupation
1 Jan 2000 - 31 Dec 2003 1 Jan 2004 - 30 Sept 2007 1 Oct 2007 - 31 Dec 2009 1 April 2010 - 31 March 2013	1 Jan 2010 - 31 March 2010

Task 2.9

The amount subject to capital gains tax for the year (after the annual exempt amount) will be **£0**

The capital loss to be carried forward to be set against future gains will be **£2,200.**

for your notes

for your notes

for your notes

for your notes